Abortion

Other Books in the Issues on Trial Series:

Abortion

Jean Leverich, Book Editor

GREENHAVEN PRESS
A part of Gale, Cengage Learning

GALE
CENGAGE Learning™

Detroit • New York • San Francisco • New Haven, Conn • Waterville, Maine • London

Christine Nasso, *Publisher*
Elizabeth Des Chenes, *Managing Editor*

© 2010 Greenhaven Press, a part of Gale, Cengage Learning

For more information, contact:
Greenhaven Press
27500 Drake Rd.
Farmington Hills, MI 48331-3535
Or you can visit our Internet site at gale.cengage.com.

For product information and technology assistance, contact us at

Gale Customer Support, 1-800-877-4253
For permission to use material from this text or product, submit all requests online at www.cengage.com/permissions

Further permissions questions can be emailed to permissionrequest@cengage.com

Articles in Greenhaven Press anthologies are often edited for length to meet page requirements. In addition, original titles of these works are changed to clearly present the main thesis and to explicitly indicate the author's opinion. Every effort is made to ensure that Greenhaven Press accurately reflects the original intent of the authors. Every effort has been made to trace the owners of copyrighted material.

Cover photograph Karen Bleier/AFP/Getty Images.

LIBRARY OF CONGRESS CATALOGING-IN-PUBLICATION DATA

Abortion / Jean Leverich, book editor.
    p. cm. -- (Issues on trial)
    Includes bibliographical references and index.
    ISBN 978-0-7377-4741-6 (hardcover)
    1. Abortion--United States--Juvenile literature. 2. Abortion--Juvenile literature.
I. Leverich, Jean.
    HQ767.5.U5A263 2010
    363.460973--dc22
                                                                    2009042500

Printed in the United States of America
1 2 3 4 5 6 7 14 13 12 11 10

Contents

Chapter 1: Legalizing Abortion

In *Roe v. Wade* (1973), the Supreme Court ruled that although the right of a woman seeking an abortion must be balanced with the state's interest in protecting maternal health and the potential life of the fetus, the right to privacy in the U.S. Constitution includes the right of women to decide whether to have children.

In his dissenting opinion Justice White argues that the Court has valued the convenience of the pregnant mother more than the existence and development of the life or potential life that she carries, and this decision creates a constitutional barrier to state efforts to protect human life.

A writer describes life before *Roe v. Wade*, when abortions were illegal in most states, and abortion itself was dangerous. She argues that the high death rate of 1930 is one way to see the prevalence of illegal abortions.

Chapter 2: Requiring Parental Notification for Minors Seeking Abortion

Chapter 3: Implementing the "Undue Burden" Standard

Chapter 4: Affirming Exceptions for Women's Health as Necessary

Chapter 5: Upholding the Partial-Birth Abortion Ban Act of 2003

In *Gonzales v. Carhart*, the Supreme Court ruled that Congress has the right to ban specific abortion procedures and that the state's interest in promoting respect for human life at all stages of the pregnancy can outweigh the woman's interest in protecting her own health and life.

Foreword

The U.S. courts have long served as a battleground for the most highly charged and contentious issues of the time. Divisive matters are often brought into the legal system by activists who feel strongly for their cause and demand an official resolution. Indeed, subjects that give rise to intense emotions or involve closely held religious or moral beliefs lay at the heart of the most polemical court rulings in history. One such case was *Brown v. Board of Education* (1954), which ended racial segregation in schools. Prior to *Brown*, the courts had held that blacks could be forced to use separate facilities as long as these facilities were equal to that of whites.

For years many groups had opposed segregation based on religious, moral, and legal grounds. Educators produced heartfelt testimony that segregated schooling greatly disadvantaged black children. They noted that in comparison to whites, blacks received a substandard education in deplorable conditions. Religious leaders such as Martin Luther King Jr. preached that the harsh treatment of blacks was immoral and unjust. Many involved in civil rights law, such as Thurgood Marshall, called for equal protection of all people under the law, as their study of the Constitution had indicated that segregation was illegal and un-American. Whatever their motivation for ending the practice, and despite the threats they received from segregationists, these ardent activists remained unwavering in their cause.

Those fighting against the integration of schools were mainly white southerners who did not believe that whites and blacks should intermingle. Blacks were subordinate to whites, they maintained, and society had to resist any attempt to break down strict color lines. Some white southerners charged that segregated schooling was *not* hindering blacks' education. For example, Virginia attorney general J. Lindsay Almond asserted, "With the help and the sympathy and the love and re-spect of the white people of the South, the colored man has risen under that educational process to a place of eminence and respect throughout the nation. It has served him well." So when the Supreme Court ruled against the segregationists in *Brown,* the South responded with vociferous cries of protest. Even government leaders criticized the decision. The governor of Arkansas, Orval Faubus, stated that he would not "be a party to any attempt to force acceptance of change to which the people are so overwhelmingly opposed." Indeed, resistance to integration was so great that when black students arrived at the formerly all-white Central High School in Arkansas, fed-eral troops had to be dispatched to quell a threatening mob of protesters.

Nevertheless, the *Brown* decision was enforced and the South integrated its schools. In this instance, the Court, while not settling the issue to everyone's satisfaction, functioned as an instrument of progress by forcing a major social change. Historian David Halberstam observes that the *Brown* ruling "deprived segregationist practices of their moral legitimacy. . . . It was therefore perhaps the single most important moment of the decade, the moment that separated the old order from the new and helped create the tumultuous era just arriving." Considered one of the most important victories for civil rights, *Brown* paved the way for challenges to racial segregation in many areas, including on public buses and in restaurants.

In examining *Brown,* it becomes apparent that the courts play an influential role—and face an arduous challenge—in shaping the debate over emotionally charged social issues. Judges must balance competing interests, keeping in mind the high stakes and intense emotions on both sides. As exempli-fied by *Brown,* judicial decisions often upset the status quo and initiate significant changes in society. Greenhaven Press's Issues on Trial series captures the controversy surrounding in-fluential court rulings and explores the social ramifications of such decisions from varying perspectives. Each anthology highlights one social issue—such as the death penalty, students' rights, or wartime civil liberties. Each volume then focuses on key historical and contemporary court cases that helped mold the issue as we know it today. The books include a compendium of primary sources—court rulings, dissents, and immediate reactions to the rulings—as well as secondary sources from experts in the field, people involved in the cases, legal analysts, and other commentators opining on the implications and legacy of the chosen cases. An annotated table of contents, an in-depth introduction, and prefaces that overview each case all provide context as readers delve into the topic at hand. To help students fully probe the subject, each volume contains book and periodical bibliographies, a comprehensive index, and a list of organizations to contact. With these features, the Issues on Trial series offers a well-rounded perspective on the courts' role in framing society's thorniest, most impassioned debates.

Introduction

O n May 31, 2009, George Tiller, one of only three physicians in the United States who specialized in late-term
abortions, was assassinated at his church in Wichita, Kansas.
This was not the first attempt on Tiller's life. In 1986 a bomb
exploded on the roof of his clinic, Women's Health Care Services, and in 1993 an antiabortion activist shot Tiller in both
arms.[1] Antiabortion groups had been trying to close down
Women's Health Care Services for almost thirty-five years,
ever since Tiller performed his first abortion in 1975.

In 2002 Operation Rescue, an antiabortion group, moved
its headquarters to Wichita in order to better target Tiller's
clinic.[2] Largely as a result of the efforts of Operation Rescue
and other antiabortion organizations, Tiller was charged with
performing nineteen illegal abortions in 1993.[3] "His is the
only abortion clinic we've never been able to close," Troy
Newman, president of Operation Rescue, told the *New York
Times* in an interview.[4] The morning after Tiller's death, however, antiabortion groups finally succeeded: Tiller's family and
coworkers decided to close the clinic. Since 1993 Tiller is the
fourth American doctor who performed late-term abortions
to have been assassinated by individuals affiliated with antiabortion organizations.

Scott Roeder, the antiabortion activist who shot Tiller at
Reformation Lutheran Church in Wichita, has stated that he is
an active member of Operation Rescue and that his motive
for killing Tiller was to protect the unborn.[5] The Federal Bu-
reau of Investigation, noting that Roeder has been visited in
jail by several convicted abortion-clinic bombers and activists
who have signed a declaration defending the murder of abortionists, has launched an investigation to determine whether
conspiracy was involved in Tiller's murder.[6] On his television
show, *The O'Reilly Factor*, Fox News commentator Bill O'Reilly

and his guest hosts mentioned Tiller on twenty-eight episodes between February 2005 and April 2009, invariably calling him "Tiller the Baby Killer" and often making incendiary comments such as "No question Dr. Tiller has blood on his hands," and "if the State of Kansas doesn't stop this man, then anybody who prevents that from happening has blood on their hands."[7]

Some antiabortion activists, such as Charmaine Yoest of Americans United for Life (AUL), have denounced the murder of Tiller: "We condemn this lawless act of violence. The foundational right to life that our work is dedicated to extends to everyone. Whoever is responsible for this reprehensible violence must be brought to justice under the law."[8] Others seemed to find the killing more justifiable. Randall Terry, founder of Operation Rescue, commented: "George Tiller was a mass-murderer. We grieve for him that he did not have time to properly prepare his soul to face God. I am more concerned that the Obama Administration will use Tiller's killing to intimidate pro-lifers into surrendering our most effective rhetoric and actions."[9] The current president of Operation Rescue, Troy Newman, called the murder of Tiller "cowardly" and stated, "Operation Rescue has worked for years through peaceful, legal means, and through the proper channels to see [Tiller] brought to justice."[10]

A *USA Today*/Gallup poll from July 2009 shows Americans nearly equally divided over the abortion issue. Of those surveyed, 47 percent of respondents identified themselves as "pro-choice" and 46 percent called themselves "pro-life."[11] In 1995, when Gallup started asking Americans their views on abortion, the split was 56 percent to 33 percent in favor of abortion rights.[12] Since the ruling in *Roe*, a majority of Americans have wanted abortion to be legal within limits. In the mid-1990s, journalist Nancy Gibbs explains, when pro-choice groups started to become a dominant voice in American culture, "only 12% believed that abortion was always wrong; now that number has nearly doubled. At each extreme, slightly more people now believe abortion should be illegal under all circumstances (23%) than legal under all circumstances (22%)."[13] As of July 2009, 70 percent of Republicans called themselves pro-life, up 10 percentage points in a single year, and although in October 2008 a Pew poll found a majority of independent voters said abortion should be legal in most cases, in May 2009 just 44 percent agreed that abortion should be legal.[14] One of the reasons why Americans' views on abortion have changed so much in recent years may be that anti-abortion groups such as Operation Rescue and Americans United for Life have effectively used the media and organized protests to get their message across. They have also used the court system both to restrict the availability of abortion and to challenge the legality of abortion by focusing on the rarest and most extreme cases of abortion, specifically late-term abortion.

Despite the increasingly polarizing rhetoric of those who feel most passionate about the abortion debate, approximately 60 percent of those who described themselves as "pro-life" in the July 2009 Gallup survey also believed that abortion should be legal in at least some circumstances.[15] This statistic indicates that many Americans are comfortable thinking of themselves as pro-life and simultaneously believing that abortion should be legal. In her *Time* magazine article "Understanding America's Shift on Abortion," Gibbs writes that "most people are neither pro-choice nor pro-life"; most people both cherish life and value choice and "trade them off with great reluctance."[16] In his commencement address at the University of Notre Dame, a Catholic institution, in May 2009, President Barack Obama recognized the complexity of the abortion debate and called for Americans to respect one another and address the possibility of common ground:

> I do not suggest that the debate surrounding abortion can or should go away. Because no matter how much we may

want to fudge it—indeed, while we know that the views of most Americans on the subject are complex and even contradictory—the fact is that at some level, the views of the two camps are irreconcilable. Each side will continue to make its case to the public with passion and conviction. But surely we can do so without reducing those with differing views to caricatures.[17]

At issue, then, is the question of how our society balances the right of women to have autonomy over their reproductive lives with the recognition that a fetus has a potential for life as well.

At the outset, when the U.S. Supreme Court decided *Roe v. Wade* (1973), the landmark case that made abortion a civil right, the Court explicitly attempted to balance the rights of women with those of the fetus. In that landmark case, the Court ruled that in the first trimester the decision to have an abortion is made by a woman and her doctor. After the first trimester and before the fetus becomes viable, the state is allowed to regulate the procedure in ways related to the pregnant woman's health. After the fetus becomes viable, or able to live on its own outside the uterus, the state can regulate and even prohibit abortion—except in cases where a doctor has determined the procedure is necessary to preserve the pregnant woman's life or health.[18] Since *Roe v. Wade* was passed in 1973, approximately 91 percent of abortions in the United States each year occur during the first trimester; only 9 percent occur during the second trimester. Less than 1 percent of 1 percent (.01 percent) of abortions are performed in the third trimester.[19]

It is these rare late-term abortions (called "intact dilation and extraction" by medical professionals and "partial-birth abortions" by antiabortion activists) about which the American public feels most ambivalent and which have been contested recently through the U.S. court system. *Stenberg v. Carhart* (2000) and *Gonzales v. Carhart* (2007) are both challenges to the legality of late-term abortions (the defendant, Leroy Carhart, worked closely with George Tiller and Warren Hern, the only other two physicians in the United States who specialized in late-term abortion). Abortion-rights opponents hope that through publicizing and outlawing late-term abortion, the criminalization of all abortions will follow. Likewise, abortion-rights supporters are concerned that the criminalization of late-term abortion will result in rendering all abortion illegal.

Since the advent of *Roe v. Wade*, the Court has been engaged in vigorous debate about to what extent access to abortion can be restricted. Several Supreme Court cases in the 1980s and 1990s, including *Ohio v. Akron Center* (1990), concerned parental notification and consent laws for minors seeking an abortion. Cases such as *Planned Parenthood of Southeastern Pennsylvania v. Casey* (1992) challenged the constitutionality of restrictive procedures such as informed consent, which required physicians to inform women about possible health risks and complications from having an abortion at least twenty-four hours before the abortion was performed; spousal notification, which required married women to sign a statement indicating that she has informed her husband of the abortion; a twenty-four-hour waiting period before a woman could receive an abortion; and a requirement that abortion providers follow onerous reporting protocols.

Throughout the history of abortion rights in America, our courts have struggled to balance a woman's right to reproductive autonomy, health, and safety with that of the life or potential life of the fetus. This anthology seeks to explore these difficult issues by looking at five of the major Supreme Court decisions related to abortion rights in America: *Roe v. Wade* (1973), *Ohio v. Akron Center* (1990), *Planned Parenthood of Southeastern Pennsylvania v. Casey* (1992), *Stenberg v. Carhart* (2000), and *Gonzales v. Carhart* (2007). By presenting the Supreme Court's decisions, the views of dissenting justices, and commentary on the impact of the cases, *Issues on Trial: Abortion* provides a comprehensive overview of an important issue with which American society continues to grapple.

Notes

1. Joe Stumpe, "Jurors Acquit Kansas Doctor in a Late-Term Abortion Case," *New York Times*, March 27, 2009.

2. Operation Rescue, "About Us: History," www.operation rescue.org.

3. Joe Stumpe, "Jurors Acquit Kansas Doctor in a Late-Term Abortion Case," *New York Times*, March 27, 2009.

4. David Barstow, "An Abortion Battle: Fought to the Death," *New York Times*, July 25, 2009.

5. *United Press International*, "Abortion Suspect Claims Membership," July 26, 2009. www.upi.com.

6. Judy L. Thomas, "George Tiller Killing: FBI Interested in Who Visits Suspect Scott Roeder in Abortion Doctor's Death," *Chicago Tribune*, August 14, 2009. www.chicagotribune.com.

7. Gabriel Winant, "O'Reilly's Campaign Against Murdered Doctor," *Salon*, May 31, 2009. www.salon.com.

8. Amy Sullivan, "Right-Wing Reactions to Tiller's Murder," *Time.com*, May 31, 2009. http://swampland.blogs.time.com.

9. Ibid.

10. *Christian News Wire*, "Operation Rescue Denounces the Killing of Abortionist Tiller," May 31, 2009. www.christian-newswire.com.

11. *United Press International*, "Poll: U.S. Equally Divided over Abortion," August 5, 2009. www.upi.com.

12. Nancy Gibbs, "Understanding America's Shift on Abortion," *Time Magazine*, May 18, 2009. www.time.com.

13. Ibid.

14. Ibid.

15. Amy Sullivan, "About That Pro-Life Majority . . . ," *Time.com*, August 13, 2009. http://swampland.blogs.time.com.

16. Nancy Gibbs, "Understanding America's Shift on Abortion," *Time Magazine*, May 18, 2009. www.time.com.

17. Barack Obama, "Remarks by the President in Commencement Address at the University of Notre Dame," May, 17, 2009. www.whitehouse.gov.

18. Harry Blackmun, majority opinion, *Roe v. Wade*, U.S. Supreme Court, 1973.

19. *FoxNews.com*, "Fast Facts: U.S. Abortion Statistics," June 17, 2003, www.foxnews.com; Department of Health and Human Services Centers for Disease Control and Prevention, "CDC's Abortion Surveillance System: FAQs," www.cdc.gov/ reproductivehealth; Guttmacher Institute, "In Brief: Facts on Induced Abortion in the United States," www.guttmacher.org.

| Legalizing Abortion

Case Overview

Roe v. Wade (1973)

Roe v. Wade is a landmark case in that it deemed abortion a fundamental right under the U.S. Constitution. According to the *Roe* decision, most state laws against abortion violated a constitutional right to privacy under the Due Process Clause of the Fourteenth Amendment.

In March 1970 a twenty-one-year-old pregnant, single woman from Dallas County, Texas, filed a class-action suit against Henry Wade, the Dallas County district attorney, on behalf of herself and "all other women similarly situated." At that time, whether a woman had access to legal abortion in the United States depended on where she lived. The woman, known by the pseudonym Jane Roe, sought a legal abortion in Texas performed by a competent, licensed physician, but Texas law permitted abortion only when a woman's life was in danger. Jane Roe, who had a tenth-grade education, was too impoverished to travel to another state where abortion was legal. Roe's attorneys, Linda Coffee and Sarah Weddington, issued a class-action suit against the state of Texas, claiming that the Texas statutes restricting abortion were unconstitutionally vague and that they violated the right of personal privacy as protected by the First, Fourth, Fifth, Ninth, and Fourteenth Amendments.

The Texas district court ruled that *Roe* had merit. The district court's decision was based primarily on the Ninth Amendment, which holds that "enumeration in the Constitution, of certain rights, shall not be construed to deny or disparage others retained by the people," as well as court precedent, including *Griswold v. Connecticut*, a 1965 Supreme Court ruling upholding the right to use contraceptives. Nevertheless, the Texas district court refused to grant an injunction against the enforcement of laws barring abortion.

In 1972 *Roe v. Wade* was heard by the Supreme Court on appeal. The Court issued its decision on January 22, 1973, with a seven-to-two majority vote in favor of *Roe*, making abortion a fundamental right under the United States Constitution. The Court determined that "arguments that Texas either has no valid interest at all in regulating the abortion decision, or no interest strong enough to support any limitation upon the woman's sole determination, are unpersuasive." Justice Harry Blackmun, who wrote the Court's opinion, stated, "We, therefore, conclude that the right of personal privacy includes the abortion decision, but that this right is not unqualified and must be considered against important state interests in regulation." Blackmun argued that "the right to privacy founded in the Fourteenth Amendment's concept of personal liberty and restriction" upon state action is "broad enough to encompass a woman's decision whether or not to terminate her pregnancy." The Fourteenth Amendment to the Constitution states, "Nor shall any State deprive any person of life, liberty, or property, without due process of law." Thus, the *Roe* majority relied on a "right of privacy" that it said was located in the Due Process Clause of the Constitution.

Writing for the majority, Blackmun asserted that the Court "need not resolve the difficult question of when life begins," only to resolve when a right to abortion exists. The Court ruled that the state cannot restrict a woman's right to an abortion during the first trimester (three months) of a pregnancy, when a fetus is not viable (cannot survive outside the womb). However, during the second trimester, the state can regulate abortion "in ways that are reasonably related to maternal health," and during the final trimester, when the fetus is viable, the state can restrict abortion "except where it is necessary, in appropriate medical judgment, for the preservation of the life or health of the mother."

One of the most controversial and politically significant Supreme Court cases in U.S. history, the *Roe v. Wade* decision initiated an ongoing national debate about whether and to what extent abortion should be legal, who should decide the legality of abortion, the role of the Supreme Court in legislation, and the role of religious and moral beliefs in the political arena. *Roe v. Wade* reshaped national politics and mobilized pro-*Roe* and anti-*Roe* movements.

> "This right of privacy ... founded in
> the Fourteenth Amendment's concept of
> personal liberty ... is broad enough to
> encompass a woman's decision whether
> or not to terminate her pregnancy."

Majority Opinion: The Fourteenth Amendment Protects a Woman's Right to Abortion

Harry Blackmun

Harry Blackmun (1908–1999) served on the Supreme Court from 1970 until 1994. Appointed to the Supreme Court by President Richard Nixon, Blackmun—a lifelong Republican and close friend of Chief Justice Warren Burger—was expected to adhere to a conservative interpretation of the Constitution. Within a short time, however, Blackmun emerged as a sympathetic liberal. His most famous opinion recognized a constitutional right to abortion in Roe v. Wade *(1973). By the time Blackmun retired, he was considered the Court's most liberal justice, though he noted that under Chief Justice William Rehnquist the Court had become more conservative.*

In the Court's 7-2 majority opinion in Roe, *Blackmun argues that the Fourteenth Amendment's guarantees of personal liberty, supported by previous decisions protecting privacy in family matters, includes a woman's right to abortion. In this ruling, the Court also recognizes that the State has valid interests in the health of the woman and the potential life of the fetus. To*

Harry Blackmun, majority opinion, *Roe v. Wade*, U.S. Supreme Court, January 22, 1973.

*address these competing rights and interests, Blackmun divides
pregnancy into trimesters—or thirds—and employs a balancing
test. During the first trimester of a pregnancy, state laws and
regulations may not interfere with a woman's right to abortion.
During the second trimester, state laws and regulations can
regulate abortion in order to protect the woman's health. During
the last trimester, when the fetus is viable—or developed enough
to survive outside the womb—state laws and regulations may
prohibit abortion except when it is necessary to preserve the life
of the woman. A landmark case,* Roe v. Wade *stipulated that a
woman's right to an abortion could only be outweighed by a
compelling state interest.*

Three reasons have been advanced to explain historically
the enactment of criminal abortion laws in the 19th century and to justify their continued existence.

It has been argued occasionally that these laws were the
product of a Victorian social concern to discourage illicit
sexual conduct. Texas, however, does not advance this justification in the present case, and it appears that no court or
commentator has taken the argument seriously. . . .

A second reason is concerned with abortion as a medical
procedure. When most criminal abortion laws were first enacted, the procedure was a hazardous one for the woman.
This was particularly true prior to the development of
antisepsis. . . . Abortion mortality was high. Even after 1900,
and perhaps until as late as the development of antibiotics in
the 1940s, standard modern techniques such as dilation and
curettage were not nearly so safe as they are today. Thus, it
has been argued that a State's real concern in enacting a criminal abortion law was to protect the pregnant woman, that is,
to restrain her from submitting to a procedure that placed her
life in serious jeopardy.

Modern medical techniques have altered this situation. . . .
Consequently, any interest of the State in protecting the

woman from an inherently hazardous procedure, except when it would be equally dangerous for her to forgo it, has largely disappeared. Of course, important state interests in the areas of health and medical standards do remain. The State has a legitimate interest in seeing to it that abortion, like any other medical procedure, is performed under circumstances that insure maximum safety for the patient. This interest obviously extends at least to the performing physician and his staff, to the facilities involved, to the availability of after-care, and to adequate provision for any complication or emergency that might arise. The prevalence of high mortality rates at illegal "abortion mills" strengthens, rather than weakens, the State's interest in regulating the conditions under which abortions are performed. Moreover, the risk to the woman increases as her pregnancy continues. Thus, the State retains a definite interest in protecting the woman's own health and safety when an abortion is proposed at a late stage of pregnancy.

The State's Interest

The third reason is the State's interest—some phrase it in terms of duty—in protecting prenatal life. Some of the argument for this justification rests on the theory that a new human life is present from the moment of conception. The State's interest and general obligation to protect life then extends, it is argued, to prenatal life. Only when the life of the pregnant mother herself is at stake, balanced against the life she carries within her, should the interest of the embryo or fetus not prevail. Logically, of course, a legitimate state interest in this area need not stand or fall on acceptance of the belief that life begins at conception or at some other point prior to live birth. In assessing the State's interest, recognition may be given to the less rigid claim that as long as at least potential life is involved, the State may assert interests beyond the protection of the pregnant woman alone.

Parties challenging state abortion laws have sharply disputed in some courts the contention that a purpose of these laws, when enacted, was to protect prenatal life. Pointing to the absence of legislative history to support the contention, they claim that most state laws were designed solely to protect the woman. Because medical advances have lessened this concern, at least with respect to abortion in early pregnancy, they argue that with respect to such abortions the laws can no longer be justified by any state interest. There is some scholarly support for this view of original purpose. The few state courts called upon to interpret their laws in the late 19th and early 20th centuries did focus on the State's interest in protecting the woman's health rather than in preserving the embryo and fetus. Proponents of this view point out that in many States, including Texas, by statute or judicial interpretation, the pregnant woman herself could not be prosecuted for self-abortion or for cooperating in an abortion performed upon her by another. They claim that adoption of the "quickening" distinction through received common law and state statutes tacitly recognizes the greater health hazards inherent in late abortion and impliedly repudiates the theory that life begins at conception.

It is with these interests, and the weight to be attached to them, that this case is concerned.

The Right of Privacy

[The] right of privacy, whether it be founded in the Fourteenth Amendment's concept of personal liberty and restrictions upon state action, as we feel it is, or, as the District Court determined, in the Ninth Amendment's reservation of rights to the people, is broad enough to encompass a woman's decision whether or not to terminate her pregnancy. The detriment that the State would impose upon the pregnant woman by denying this choice altogether is apparent. Specific and direct harm medically diagnosable even in early pregnancy may be involved. Maternity, or additional offspring, may force upon the woman a distressful life and future. Psychological harm may be imminent. Mental and physical health may be taxed by child care. There is also the distress, for all concerned, associated with the unwanted child, and there is the problem of bringing a child into a family already unable, psychologically and otherwise, to care for it. In other cases, as in this one, the additional difficulties and continuing stigma of unwed motherhood may be involved. All these are factors the woman and her responsible physician necessarily will consider in consultation.

On the basis of elements such as these, appellant and some amici argue that the woman's right is absolute and that she is entitled to terminate her pregnancy at whatever time, in whatever way, and for whatever reason she alone chooses. With this we do not agree. Appellant's arguments that Texas either has no valid interest at all in regulating the abortion decision, or no interest strong enough to support any limitation upon the woman's sole determination, are unpersuasive. The Court's decisions recognizing a right of privacy also acknowledge that some state regulation in areas protected by that right is appropriate. As noted above, a State may properly assert important interests in safeguarding health, in maintaining medical standards, and in protecting potential life. At some point in pregnancy, these respective interests become sufficiently compelling to sustain regulation of the factors that govern the abortion decision. The privacy right involved, therefore, cannot be said to be absolute. . . .

We, therefore, conclude that the right of personal privacy includes the abortion decision, but that this right is not unqualified and must be considered against important state interests in regulation.

We note that those federal and state courts that have recently considered abortion law challenges have reached the same conclusion. A majority, in addition to the District Court in the present case, have held state laws unconstitutional, at least in part, because of vagueness or because of overbreadth and abridgment of rights. . . .

Right to Privacy Covers Abortion

Although the results are divided, most of these courts have agreed that the right of privacy, however based, is broad enough to cover the abortion decision; that the right, nonetheless, is not absolute and is subject to some limitations; and that at some point the state interests as to protection of health, medical standards, and prenatal life, become dominant. We agree with this approach.

Where certain "fundamental rights" are involved, the Court has held that regulation limiting these rights may be justified only by a "compelling state interest," and that legislative enactments must be narrowly drawn to express only the legitimate state interests at stake.

In the recent abortion cases, . . . courts have recognized these principles. Those striking down state laws have generally scrutinized the state's interests in protecting health and potential life, and have concluded that neither interest justified broad limitations on the reasons for which a physician and his pregnant patient might decide that she should have an abortion in the early stages of pregnancy. Courts sustaining state laws have held that the State's determinations to protect health or prenatal life are dominant and constitutionally justifiable.

"Person" Excludes Unborn

The District Court held that the appellee failed to meet his burden of demonstrating that the Texas statute's infringement upon Roe's rights was necessary to support a compelling state interest, and that, although the appellee presented "several compelling justifications for state presence in the area of abortions," the statutes outstripped these justifications and swept "far beyond any areas of compelling state interest." Appellant and appellee both contest that holding. Appellant, as has been indicated, claims an absolute right that bars any state imposition of criminal penalties in the area. Appellee argues that the State's determination to recognize and protect prenatal life from and after conception constitutes a compelling state interest. As noted above, we do not agree fully with either formulation.

A. The appellee and certain amici argue that the fetus is a "person" within the language and meaning of the Fourteenth Amendment. In support of this, they outline at length and in detail the well-known facts of fetal development. If this suggestion of personhood is established, the appellant's case, of course, collapses, for the fetus' right to life would then be guaranteed specifically by the Amendment. The appellant conceded as much on reargument. On the other hand, the appellee conceded on reargument that no case could be cited that holds that a fetus is a person within the meaning of the Fourteenth Amendment.

The Constitution does not define "person" in so many words. Section 1 of the Fourteenth Amendment contains three references to "person." The first, in defining "citizens," speaks of "persons born or naturalized in the United States." The word also appears both in the Due Process Clause and in the Equal Protection Clause. "Person" is used in other places in the Constitution. . . .

But in nearly all these instances, the use of the word is such that it has application only postnatally. None indicates, with any assurance, that it has any possible pre-natal application.

All this, together with our observation, that throughout the major portion of the 19th century prevailing legal abortion practices were far freer than they are today, persuades us that the word "person," as used in the Fourteenth Amendment, does not include the unborn. This is in accord with the results reached in those few cases where the issue has been squarely presented. . . .

A Difficult Question

B. The pregnant woman cannot be isolated in her privacy. She carries an embryo and, later, a fetus, if one accepts the medical definitions of the developing young in the human uterus. The situation therefore is inherently different from marital intimacy, or bedroom possession of obscene material, or marriage, or procreation, or education. . . . As we have intimated above, it is reasonable and appropriate for a State to decide that at some point in time another interest, that of health of the mother or that of potential human life, becomes significantly involved. The woman's privacy is no longer sole and any right of privacy she possesses must be measured accordingly.

Texas urges that, apart from the Fourteenth Amendment, life begins at conception and is present throughout pregnancy, and that, therefore, the State has a compelling interest in protecting that life from and after conception. We need not resolve the difficult question of when life begins. When those trained in the respective disciplines of medicine, philosophy, and theology are unable to arrive at any consensus, the judiciary, at this point in the development of man's knowledge, is not in a position to speculate as to the answer.

It should be sufficient to note briefly the wide divergence of thinking on this most sensitive and difficult question. There has always been strong support for the view that life does not begin until live birth. This was the belief of the Stoics [ancient Greek philosophers]. It appears to be the predominant, though not the unanimous, attitude of the Jewish faith. It may be taken to represent also the position of a large segment of the Protestant community, insofar as that can be ascertained; organized groups that have taken a formal position on the abortion issue have generally regarded abortion as a matter for the conscience of the individual and her family. As we have noted, the common law found greater significance in quickening. Physicians and their scientific colleagues have regarded that event with less interest and have tended to focus either upon conception, upon live birth, or upon the interim point at which the fetus becomes "viable," that is, potentially able to live outside the mother's womb, albeit with artificial aid. Viability is usually placed at about seven months (28 weeks) but may occur earlier, even at 24 weeks. . . .

In areas other than criminal abortion, the law has been reluctant to endorse any theory that life, as we recognize it, begins before live birth or to accord legal rights to the unborn except in narrowly defined situations and except when the rights are contingent upon live birth. For example, the traditional rule of tort law denied recovery for prenatal injuries even though the child was born alive. That rule has been changed in almost every jurisdiction. In most States, recovery is said to be permitted only if the fetus was viable, or at least quick, when the injuries were sustained, though few courts have squarely so held. In a recent development, generally opposed by the commentators, some States permit the parents of a stillborn child to maintain an action for wrongful death because of prenatal injuries. Such an action, however, would appear to be one to vindicate the parents' interest and is thus consistent with the view that the fetus, at most, represents only the potentiality of life. Similarly, unborn children have been recognized as acquiring rights or interests by way of inheritance or other devolution of property, and have been represented by guardians ad litem. Perfection of the interests involved, again, has generally been contingent upon live birth. In short, the unborn have never been recognized in the law as persons in the whole sense. . . .

A Compelling Interest

[T]he State does have an important and legitimate interest in preserving and protecting the health of the pregnant woman, whether she be a resident of the State or a nonresident who seeks medical consultation and treatment there, and that it has still another important and legitimate interest in protecting the potentiality of human life. These interests are separate and distinct. Each grows in substantiality as the woman approaches term and, at a point during pregnancy, each becomes "compelling."

With respect to the State's important and legitimate interest in the health of the mother, the "compelling" point, in the light of present medical knowledge, is at approximately the end of the first trimester. This is so because of the now-established medical fact that until the end of the first trimester mortality in abortion may be less than mortality in normal childbirth. It follows that, from and after this point, a State may regulate the abortion procedure to the extent that the regulation reasonably relates to the preservation and protection of maternal health. Examples of permissible state regulation in this area are requirements as to the qualifications of the person who is to perform the abortion; as to the licensure of that person; as to the facility in which the procedure is to be performed, that is, whether it must be a hospital or may be a clinic or some other place of less-than-hospital status; as to the licensing of the facility; and the like.

This means, on the other hand, that, for the period of pregnancy prior to this "compelling" point, the attending physician, in consultation with his patient, is free to determine, without regulation by the State, that, in his medical judgment, the patient's pregnancy should be terminated. If that decision is reached, the judgment may be effectuated by an abortion free of interference by the State.

With respect to the State's important and legitimate interest in potential life, the "compelling" point is at viability. This is so because the fetus then presumably has the capability of meaningful life outside the mother's womb. State regulation protective of fetal life after viability thus has both logical and biological justifications. If the State is interested in protecting fetal life after viability, it may go so far as to proscribe abortion during that period, except when it is necessary to preserve the life or health of the mother. . . .

Balancing the Concerns

To summarize . . . :

A state criminal abortion statute of the current Texas type, that excepts from criminality only a life-saving procedure on behalf of the mother, without regard to pregnancy stage and without recognition of the other interests involved, is violative of the Due Process Clause of the Fourteenth Amendment.

(a) For the stage prior to approximately the end of the first trimester, the abortion decision and its effectuation must be left to the medical judgment of the pregnant woman's attending physician.

(b) For the stage subsequent to approximately the end of the first trimester, the State, in promoting its interest in the health of the mother, may, if it chooses, regulate the abortion procedure in ways that are reasonably related to maternal health.

(c) For the stage subsequent to viability, the State in promoting its interest in the potentiality of human life may, if it chooses, regulate, and even proscribe, abortion except where it is necessary, in appropriate medical judgment, for the preservation of the life or health of the mother.

This holding, we feel, is consistent with the relative weights of the respective interests involved, with the lessons and examples of medical and legal history, with the lenity of the common law, and with the demands of the profound problems of the present day. The decision leaves the State free to place increasing restrictions on abortion as the period of pregnancy lengthens, so long as those restrictions are tailored to the recognized state interests. The decision vindicates the right of the physician to administer medical treatment according to his professional judgment up to the points where important state interests provide compelling justifications for intervention. Up to those points; the abortion decision in all its aspects is inherently, and primarily, a medical decision, and basic responsibility for it must rest with the physician. If an individual practitioner abuses the privilege of exercising proper medical judgment, the usual remedies, judicial and intra-professional, are available.

> "The Court apparently values the convenience of the pregnant mother more than the continued existence and development of the life or potential life that she carries."

Dissenting Opinion: The Life of the Woman Should Not Be More Valued than the Life of the Fetus

Byron White

Byron White (1917–2002) was perhaps the only Supreme Court justice to play professional football; he played for the Pittsburgh Pirates (now Steelers) before studying at Oxford University on a Rhodes Scholarship. Appointed to the Supreme Court in 1962 by President John F. Kennedy, White wrote 994 opinions before retiring in 1993. As a justice, White often took a narrow, fact-specific view of cases before the Court and generally refused to make broad pronouncements on constitutional doctrine.

Roe v. Wade (1973) was argued at the same time as a related case, Doe v. Bolton *(1973), in which the Supreme Court struck down certain Georgia abortion restrictions. Two justices, White and William Rehnquist, dissented in both cases. In his scathing dissent in* Doe, *White asserts that there is nothing in the language or history of the Constitution to support the Court's judgment and that the Court has overreached in overriding existing state abortion statutes. Furthermore, White contends, the Court's decision creates a "constitutional barrier" to state efforts*

Byron White, dissenting opinion, *Doe v. Bolton*, U.S. Supreme Court, January 22, 1973.

to protect human life. He decries a ruling that "values the convenience of the pregnant mother more than the continued existence and development of the life or potential life that she carries."

At the heart of the controversy in these cases are those recurring pregnancies that pose no danger whatsoever to the life or health of the mother but are, nevertheless, unwanted for any one or more of a variety of reasons—convenience, family planning, economics, dislike of children, the embarrassment of illegitimacy, etc. The common claim before us is that for any one of such reasons, or for no reason at all, and without asserting or claiming any threat to life or health, any woman is entitled to an abortion at her request if she is able to find a medical advisor willing to undertake the procedure.

The Court for the most part sustains this position: During the period prior to the time the fetus becomes viable, the Constitution of the United States values the convenience, whim, or caprice of the putative mother more than the life or potential life of the fetus; the Constitution, therefore, guarantees the right to an abortion as against any state law or policy seeking to protect the fetus from an abortion not prompted by more compelling reasons of the mother.

No Constitutional Right to Abortion

With all due respect, I dissent. I find nothing in the language or history of the Constitution to support the Court's judgment. The Court simply fashions and announces a new constitutional right for pregnant mothers and, with scarcely any reason or authority for its action, invests that right with sufficient substance to override most existing state abortion statutes. The upshot is that the people and the legislatures of the 50 States are constitutionally disentitled to weigh the relative importance of the continued existence and development of the fetus, on the one hand, against a spectrum of possible impacts on the mother, on the other hand. As an exercise of raw judicial power, the Court perhaps has authority to do what it does today; but in my view its judgment is an improvident and extravagant exercise of the power of judicial review that the Constitution extends to this Court.

The Court apparently values the convenience of the pregnant mother more than the continued existence and development of the life or potential life that she carries. Whether or not I might agree with that marshaling of values, I can in no event join the Court's judgment because I find no constitutional warrant for imposing such an order of priorities on the people and legislatures of the States. In a sensitive area such as this, involving as it does issues over which reasonable men may easily and heatedly differ, I cannot accept the Court's exercise of its clear power of choice by interposing a constitutional barrier to state efforts to protect human life and by investing mothers and doctors with the constitutionally protected right to exterminate it. This issue, for the most part, should be left with the people and to the political processes the people have devised to govern their affairs.

It is my view, therefore, that the Texas statute is not constitutionally infirm because it denies abortions to those who seek to serve only their convenience rather than to protect their life or health. Nor is this plaintiff, who claims no threat to her mental or physical health, entitled to assert the possible rights of those women ... whose pregnancy assertedly implicates their health. This ... dictates reversal of the judgment of the District Court.

> "One stark indication of the prevalence
> of illegal abortion was the death toll."

Abortion Before *Roe v. Wade* Was Dangerous

Rachel Benson Gold

Rachel Benson Gold is currently the Director of Policy Analysis and Washington Office Operations at the Guttmacher Institute.

In the following viewpoint, Gold describes the events prior to Roe v. Wade. Although abortions were illegal in most states, they were relatively common. Gold argues that the high death rate of 1930 is one way to see the prevalence of illegal abortions. She believes that by legalizing abortion, Roe v. Wade provided a much safer way for women to have abortions and eliminate the infections and deaths that accompanied illegal abortions.

The Supreme Court did not "invent" legal abortion, much less abortion itself, when it handed down its historic *Roe v. Wade* decision in 1973. Abortion, both legal and illegal, had long been part of life in America. Indeed, the legal status of abortion has passed through several distinct phases in American history. Generally permitted at the nation's founding and for several decades thereafter, the procedure was made illegal under most circumstances in most states beginning in the mid-1800s. In the 1960s, states began reforming their strict antiabortion laws, so that when the Supreme Court made abortion legal nationwide, legal abortions were already available in 17 states under a range of circumstances beyond those necessary to save a woman's life.

Rachel Benson Gold, "Lessons from Before Roe: Will Past Be Prologue?" *The Guttmacher Report on Public Policy*, vol. 6, March 2003. Reproduced by permission.

But regardless of the legal status of abortion, its fundamental underlying cause—unintended pregnancy—has been a continuing reality for American women. In the 1960s, researchers from Princeton University estimated that almost one in three Americans (32%) who wanted no more children were likely to have at least one unintended pregnancy before the end of their childbearing years; more than six in 10 Americans (62%) wanting children at some point in the future were likely to have experienced at least one unintended pregnancy.

While the problem of unintended pregnancy spanned all strata of society, the choices available to women varied before *Roe*. At best, these choices could be demeaning and humiliating, and at worst, they could lead to injury and death. Women with financial means had some, albeit very limited, recourse to a legal abortion; less affluent women, who disproportionately were young and members of minority groups, had few options aside from a dangerous illegal procedure.

Illegal Abortions Were Common and Dangerous

Estimates of the number of illegal abortions in the 1950s and 1960s ranged from 200,000 to 1.2 million per year. One analysis, extrapolating from data from North Carolina, concluded that an estimated 829,000 illegal or self-induced abortions occurred in 1967.

One stark indication of the prevalence of illegal abortion was the death toll. In 1930, abortion was listed as the official cause of death for almost 2,700 women—nearly one-fifth (18%) of maternal deaths recorded in that year. The death toll had declined to just under 1,700 by 1940, and to just over 300 by 1950 (most likely because of the introduction of antibiotics in the 1940s, which permitted more effective treatment of the infections that frequently developed after illegal abortion). By 1965, the number of deaths due to illegal abortion had fallen to just under 200, but illegal abortion still accounted for 17%

of all deaths attributed to pregnancy and childbirth that year. And these are just the number that were officially reported; the actual number was likely much higher.

Poor women and their families were disproportionately impacted. A study of low-income women in New York City in the 1960s found that almost one in 10 (8%) had ever attempted to terminate a pregnancy by illegal abortion; almost four in 10 (38%) said that a friend, relative or acquaintance had attempted to obtain an abortion. Of the low-income women in that study who said they had had an abortion, eight in 10 (77%) said that they had attempted a self-induced procedure, with only 2% saying that a physician had been involved in any way.

These women paid a steep price for illegal procedures. In 1962 alone, nearly 1,600 women were admitted to Harlem Hospital Center in New York City for incomplete abortions, which was one abortion-related hospital admission for every 42 deliveries at that hospital that year. In 1968, the University of Southern California Los Angeles County Medical Center, another large public facility serving primarily indigent patients, admitted 701 women with septic abortions, one admission for every 14 deliveries.

A clear racial disparity is evident in the data of mortality because of illegal abortion: In New York City in the early 1960s, one in four childbirth-related deaths among white women was due to abortion; in comparison, abortion accounted for one in two childbirth-related deaths among nonwhite and Puerto Rican women.

Even in the early 1970s, when abortion was legal in some states, a legal abortion was simply out of reach for many. Minority women suffered the most: The Centers for Disease Control and Prevention estimates that in 1972 alone, 130,000 women obtained illegal or self-induced procedures, 39 of whom died. Furthermore, from 1972 to 1974, the mortality rate due to illegal abortion for nonwhite women was 12 times that for white women.

Navigating the System

Although legal abortions were largely unavailable until the years just before *Roe*, some women were always able to obtain the necessary approval for an abortion under the requirements of their state law. In most states, until just before 1973, this meant demonstrating that a woman's life would be endangered if she carried her pregnancy to term. In some states, especially between 1967 and 1973, a woman also could receive approval for an abortion if it were deemed necessary to protect her physical or mental health, or if the pregnancy had resulted from rape or incest.

Even so, the process to obtain approval for a legal abortion could be arduous. In many states, it involved securing the approval of a standing hospital committee established specifically to review abortion requests. Either as a matter of state law or hospital policy, these committees frequently required that additional physicians examine the woman to corroborate her own physician's finding that an abortion was necessary to protect her life or physical health. Likewise, a licensed psychiatrist might be required to second the judgment of a woman's doctor that an abortion was necessary on mental health grounds, or a law enforcement officer might be required to certify that the woman had reported being sexually assaulted.

Contemporaneous accounts noted that a woman's ability to navigate this process successfully generally required having a long-standing relationship with a physician. In practice, this meant that the option was only available to those who were able to pay for the review process, in addition to the procedure itself. One study of the 2,775 so-called therapeutic abortions at private, not-for-profit hospitals in New York City between 1951 and 1962 found that 88% were to patients of private physicians, rather than ward patients served by the hospital staff. The abortion to live-birth ratio for white women was five times that of nonwhite women, and 26 times that of Puerto Rican women.

Travelling for Abortion

In the late 1960s, an alternative to obtaining committee approval emerged for women seeking a legal abortion, but once again, only for those with considerable financial resources. In 1967, England liberalized its abortion law to permit any woman to have an abortion with the written consent of two physicians. More than 600 American women made the trip to the United Kingdom during the last three months of 1969 alone; by 1970, package deals (including round-trip airfare, passports, vaccination, transportation to and from the airport and lodging and meals for four days, in addition to the procedure itself) were advertised in the popular media.

Beginning in 1970, four states—Alaska, Hawaii, New York and Washington—also repealed their antiabortion statutes, and generally allowed licensed physicians to perform abortions on request before fetal viability. Alaska, Hawaii and Washington required a woman seeking an abortion to be a resident of the state for at least 30 days prior to the procedure; New York did not include a residency requirement, which put it on the map as an option for the affluent.

The year before the Supreme Court's decision in *Roe v. Wade*, just over 100,000 women left their own state to obtain a legal abortion in New York City. According to an analysis by The Alan Guttmacher Institute, an estimated 50,000 women traveled more than 500 miles to obtain a legal abortion in New York City; nearly 7,000 women traveled more than 1,000 miles, and some 250 traveled more than 2,000 miles, from places as far as Arizona, Idaho and Nevada.

Data from the New York City Department of Health confirm that this option, as difficult as it was, was really only available to the small proportion of women who were able to pay for the procedure plus the expense of travel and lodging. (Nonresidents were not eligible for either Medicaid-covered care in New York or care from the state's public hospitals.) While eight in 10 nonresidents obtaining abortions in the city between July 1971 and July 1972 were white, seven in 10 city residents who underwent the procedure during that time were nonwhite.

A serious consequence of having to travel long distances to obtain an abortion was the resulting delay in having the procedure performed, which could raise the risk of complications for the woman. No more than 10% of New York City residents who had an abortion in the city in 1972 did so after the 12th week of pregnancy; in contrast, 23% of women from nonneighboring states who had an abortion in New York City did so after the 12th week.

Moreover, a woman who traveled long distances to obtain an abortion not only had to undergo the rigors of travel shortly after a surgical procedure but also was precluded from continuity in her medical care if she needed follow-up services. By the time a complication occurred, an out-of-state woman might already be home, where she would be unable to receive care from the physician who performed the abortion and, perhaps, from any physician with significant abortion experience.

Learning from History

By making abortion legal nationwide, *Roe v. Wade* has had a dramatic impact on the health and well-being of American women. Deaths from abortion have plummeted, and are now a rarity. In addition, women have been able to have abortions earlier in pregnancy when the procedure is safest: The proportion of abortions obtained early in the first trimester has risen from 20% in 1970 to 56% in 1998. These public health accomplishments may now be seriously threatened.

Supporters of legal abortion face the bleakest political landscape in recent history. Congress is poised to pass legislation criminalizing some abortion procedures (termed "partial-birth" abortion) even when they are performed prior to fetal viability and when they are deemed by the physician to be in the best interest of the woman's health; by doing so, the Partial-Birth Abortion Ban Act takes direct aim at the basic principles underlying *Roe*. In the likely event the measure is passed, signed by the president and then challenged, its fate will be decided by a Supreme Court whose balance may have been tipped by the most doggedly antiabortion administration in history. In short, it is more possible than at any time in the past 30 years that the legal status of abortion is about to undergo a major change.

Should the Supreme Court overturn *Roe* and return the fundamental question of abortion's legality to the states, NARAL Pro-Choice America estimates that abortion could be made illegal in 17 states. In that light, the years before *Roe* offer something of a cautionary tale. Granted, it is by no means a given that the precise dimensions of the public health situation that existed before 1973 would reappear. However, it must be considered extremely likely that such an overhaul of U.S. abortion jurisprudence would lead to the reestablishment of a two-tiered system in which options available to a woman confronting an unintended pregnancy would be largely determined by her socioeconomic status. Such a system has proved to be deleterious to the health of women, especially those who are disadvantaged, and is something that many had hoped would have been long consigned to the history books.

Legal Status of Abortion Throughout American History

Legal abortion has been part of American life for much of the nation's history. Under English common law, the cornerstone of American jurisprudence, abortions performed prior to "quickening" (the first perceptible fetal movement, which usually occurs after the fourth month of pregnancy) were not criminal offenses. With no state enacting specific legislation during nearly the first third of the nation's history, this traditional principle prevailed. The medical literature of the day, both popular and professional, included frequent references to methods of abortion.

In the mid-1800s, Massachusetts enacted the first state law making abortion or attempted abortion at any point in pregnancy a criminal offense. By the turn of the century, almost all states had followed suit. In the early 1960s, only Pennsylvania prohibited all abortions, but 44 other states only allowed abortion when the woman's life would be endangered if she carried the pregnancy to term. Alabama, Colorado, New Mexico, Massachusetts and the District of Columbia permitted abortion if the life or physical health of the woman was in jeopardy; Mississippi allowed abortions in case of life endangerment or rape.

Violating these laws could have serious legal consequences, not only for the provider but potentially for others as well. In nine states, the laws considered it a criminal offense to aid, assist, abet or counsel a woman in obtaining an illegal abortion. Fourteen states explicitly made obtaining an abortion, as well as performing one, a crime. Women were rarely convicted for having an abortion; instead, the threat of prosecution often was used to encourage them to testify against the provider.

One of the first national calls for a change in abortion law came in 1962 from the American Law Institute (ALI)—a prestigious panel of lawyers, scholars and jurists that develops model statutes on a range of topics—with the publication of its "Model Penal Code on Abortion," which called for abortion to be legal when the pregnant woman's life or health would be at risk if the pregnancy were carried to term, when the pregnancy resulted from rape or incest, or when the fetus had a severe defect.

In 1967, Colorado became the first state to reform its abortion law based on the ALI recommendation. The new Colorado statute permitted abortions if the pregnant woman's life or physical or mental health were endangered, if the fetus would be born with a severe physical or mental defect, or if the pregnancy had resulted from rape or incest. Other states began to follow suit, and by 1972, 13 states had so-called ALI statutes. Meanwhile, four states repealed their antiabortion laws completely, substituting statutes permitting abortions that were judged to be necessary by a woman and her physician. By 1973, when the Supreme Court handed down its decision in *Roe*, abortion reform legislation had been introduced in all but five states.

> "New technologies that have the potential to expand abortion access and to facilitate earlier abortions ... are an important [public health] development."

Roe v. Wade Has Provided Advances in Public Health

Carole Joffe

Carole Joffe is a professor of sociology at the University of California at Davis. She is the author of three books, including Doctors of Conscience: The Struggle to Provide Abortion Before and After *Roe v. Wade (1995), as well as many scholarly articles. She also writes frequently about reproductive health and reproductive politics in such outlets as the* Washington Post, *the* Los Angeles Times, Salon, *the* Philadelphia Inquirer, *and the* San Francisco Chronicle.

In the following viewpoint, Joffe notes that thirty years after the Roe v. Wade *decision, which legalized abortion in the United States, there are fewer abortion providers, a hostile regulatory environment, limits to international family planning, and an organized antiabortion movement. Nevertheless, she contends, advances in technology, medical training, and public health mobilization give reason to believe that more doctors and hospitals will be able and willing to provide abortion in the future.*

A t the 30th anniversary of *Roe v. Wade*, it is time for the inevitable stocktaking by the prochoice movement. But rather than celebrating such a landmark anniversary, many in

Carole Joffe, "*Roe v. Wade* at 30: What Are the Prospects for Abortion Provision?" *Perspectives on Sexual and Reproductive Health*, vol. 35, January/February 2003, pp. 29–33. Reproduced by permission.

the movement appear grimly relieved that abortion is still legal at all in the United States. It was not supposed to be like this. Acknowledging such a milestone *should* involve looking back on the considerable advances in public health that resulted from legalization—the dramatic reductions in rates of abortion-related death and injury, and the enormous changes in American women's lives that were enabled, in considerable part, by the availability of reliable and safe abortion services. Instead, the story is about how abortion emerged as one of the most divisive issues in American society, the target of a nonstop assault by its foes in Congress and in the streets— and seemingly everywhere in between.

As of this writing, in the immediate aftermath of the November 2002 elections, which gave Republicans control of both the House and the Senate, the situation looks particularly bleak. Antiabortion forces have introduced yet another "partial-birth abortion" bill (although the Supreme Court has found nearly identical bans unconstitutional); President [George W.] Bush has overruled his own State Department's recommendations by refusing to allow funding for international family planning; contentious hearings have been held for Bush judicial nominees seemingly chosen for their antiabortion record; and the antiabortion movement has trumpeted its newest tactic of videotaping patients as they enter abortion clinics and then posting the tapes on the Internet. And of course, the prochoice movement trembles while it waits for the proverbial other shoe to drop: When will George W. Bush have the opportunity to nominate a Supreme Court justice who could provide the fifth vote to overturn *Roe* altogether?

Abortion Providers Harassed

A similar feeling that things have not turned out the way they were supposed to pervades the medical wing of the prochoice movement. Certainly no physician could have predicted that providers would be harassed and violently attacked—including seven who were gunned down by antiabortion terrorists—in the years after *Roe*. Just before *Roe*, in 1972, 100 professors of obstetrics and gynecology wrote to their colleagues of the necessity to prepare for abortion's imminent legalization. Their statement confidently predicted that "if only half of the 20,000 obstetricians in this country do abortions, they can do a million a year, at a rate of two per physician per week. . . . Independent clinics will probably not be necessary if all hospitals cooperate in handling their proportionate share of these cases."

It is deeply frustrating to read these words today. Far from half of the some 48,000 practicing obstetrician-gynecologists provide abortions, although the precise proportion is unknown. Currently only 1,819 known facilities provide abortions—46% of these sites are clinics, 33% are hospitals and 21% physicians' offices. Hospitals provide fewer than 5% of all abortions. The absence of a provider in some 87% of U.S. counties has become the mantra of the beleaguered prochoice movement. . . .

Promising Developments

Amid the usual signs of siege, however, several promising developments may herald a turning point. First, there is a new-found commitment to abortion training in key locales, which has received national attention. For instance, all public hospitals that offer obstetrics and gynecology residencies in New York City must now provide training in abortion methods, and the governor of California has signed into law, as part of a package of prochoice legislation, a similar measure covering state-supported residencies in California.

Second, in a field that had seen few technological innovations since the introduction of the vacuum suction machine in the late 1960s, several new technologies became available in the mid-1990s. "Medical" abortion—that is, abortion via a drug rather than the more familiar "surgical" abortion—came to the United States in two forms. First, mifepristone, also known as RU 486, began U.S. clinical trials in 1996, and the Food and Drug Administration (FDA) approved it for general use as a method of medical abortion in 2000. Second, in the mid-1990s, many U.S. physicians began to use methotrexate, a cancer drug, for the off-label purpose of pregnancy termination.

Simultaneously, manual vacuum aspiration, a technology that permits very early abortion in a medical office setting, also reemerged. Its sudden and unexpected reappearance in the United States may have been an unanticipated result of the extended delay in FDA approval of mifepristone for general use: Some 12 years passed between French approval in 1988 and U.S. approval in 2000; during that period, both health care providers and patients became attracted to the prospect of very early terminations.

More Contraceptive Options

The ability to act as quickly as possible has been enhanced by the widespread availability of reliable and affordable pregnancy test kits, which can detect a pregnancy as soon as seven days after fertilization. Taken together, these developments raise the prospect of changing the cultural and political landscape surrounding reproductive health decisions. Women have more contraceptive options, which have succeeded in reducing the need for abortion in the first place, and they have the ability to detect a pregnancy sooner. Moreover, both medical abortion and manual vacuum aspiration offer the possibility of earlier abortions compared with surgical abortion. Given that abortion is generally more acceptable—among both the public and providers—the earlier it takes place, these new technologies together could eventually "change the conversation" surrounding abortion, as one observer put it.

Of all these developments, perhaps none has raised more hope among abortion rights supporters than mifepristone, because it may directly affect the problem of accessibility. Since its provision does not require surgical training, the new regimen has a far wider range of potential providers—e.g., primary care physicians, family practice physicians, internists and adolescent health specialists. Moreover, because the key task involves effective counseling rather than surgical skill, advanced-practice clinicians (medical professionals other than doctors, such as physician assistants, midwives and nurse practitioners) may be logical providers. Mifepristone also raises prospects for the diffusion of abortion care to settings that extend beyond the freestanding clinic, where most U.S. procedures now take place.

An unusual amount of political mobilization by prochoice medical organizations, both old and new, is another positive sign. Although groups advocating the expansion of abortion training and access largely target the medical community itself, they have also directed public relations offensives highlighting abortion's public health benefits to the general population. . . .

Importance of Training and Research

The creation of several new programs within leading medical institutions to promote abortion training and research is yet another step forward. . . . Given the historic antipathy toward abortion providers in much of mainstream medicine, these programs in first-tier medical schools will presumably increase the legitimacy of the field.

In most branches of medicine, such positive developments might reasonably be expected to translate smoothly into more providers, a wider geographic range of services and increased accessibility for patients. In the highly politicized world of abortion, of course, nothing works smoothly. And despite the undeniable evidence of a newly energized prochoice movement, especially in the realm of training, many obstacles remain to seeing these efforts pay off in increased numbers of abortion providers and facilities.

To start, providers of surgical abortion face no shortage of problems—for example, the list includes onerous legal restrictions, uncooperative landlords and vendors, disapproving colleagues and the ever-present threat of harassment and violence. But most surgical abortions take place in freestanding clinics or office practices that do a high volume of procedures. Such facilities typically have specialized staff on-site to manage these problems and lawyers on call to handle the myriad legal issues that arise.

Thus, the many obstacles that pervade abortion provision are perhaps clearest among the pool of potential medical abortion providers, those who will ideally incorporate abortion into a primary care practice and perform relatively few procedures. This is precisely the group on whom the movement has pinned high hopes for expanded access.

Obstacles for Medical Professionals

Briefly, here are some of the obstacles that these professionals have to overcome.

Malpractice and Insurance Issues: Malpractice insurance is a major stumbling block, particularly for providers other than obstetrician-gynecologists, who will likely see their premiums soar once they add abortion to their practice. . . .

Legal and Regulatory Environment: The new provider of medical abortion must become conversant with a legal and regulatory environment that is like no other in contemporary medicine. For example, the provider must know about such regulations as parental consent laws, 24-hour waiting periods, abortion reporting requirements and rules governing the handling of fetal tissue. While ultimately the courts may decide that some aspects of the laws that regulate surgical abortion do not apply to medical abortion, the best legal thinking counsels would-be providers to assume that currently they do. Moreover, new providers of medical abortion will have to contend with so-called TRAP (Targeted Regulations of Abortion Providers) laws, which place additional restrictions on the facilities or practices of physicians who provide abortion. Some of these laws' features are patently absurd in the context of medical abortion—for example, specifications for the widths of doorways.

Restrictive Contracts: The potential provider of medical abortion may likely come up against employer contract restrictions that prohibit abortion. Many instances of restrictions on abortion have been reported, even when Catholic facilities have not been involved. For example, some group practices prohibit abortion provision out of fear of controversy; these restrictions can even extend to prohibiting a doctor from providing abortions off-site at a freestanding clinic. Similarly, some landlords of private offices prohibit abortions on their property, because of personal objections or fears of picketing and disruption.

Complexities of the Mifepristone Regimen: A number of features of the mifepristone regimen make it quite costly—in terms of time, energy and sometimes money—for a new provider. First, whereas most approved drugs can be obtained by the patient from a pharmacist, the unusual terms of the FDA's approval of mifepristone stipulate that the prescribing physician order it directly. For some physicians, especially those planning to offer only a few medical abortions, this means paying in advance for more medication than may be needed and risking expiration of any unused drugs on hand. At the same time, getting hold of this drug has proved surprisingly cumbersome for individual doctors who work in hospital-based residency programs, who depend on drugs that are ordered by a central pharmacy. . . .

Surely, these obstacles can be expected to lessen over time. Although the uptake of medical abortion by new providers has been slower than some had anticipated, mifepristone is now well integrated into the services of veteran abortion providers and has increased access to abortion overall. For example, a number of Planned Parenthood clinics that had not provided surgical abortion now offer medical abortion, and clinics that offer both procedures have found it easier to integrate medical abortions into their schedules than surgical abortions. Presumably, malpractice insurance and reimbursement problems will be solved by creative new solutions. The greatest obstacle to expanding abortion services, however, may be the medical culture itself—one that supports legal abortion, but has always stayed at arm's length from actual providers and services. . . .

Grounds for Concern and Optimism

In assessing where the medical community now stands vis-à-vis abortion after 30 years of legalization, one can see strong parallels with the position of American society as a whole. The antiabortion movement has not succeeded in turning people against legal abortion; polls repeatedly show that a majority do not want *Roe v. Wade* overturned. Nonetheless, the antiabortion movement has succeeded in making many people feel very ambivalent about abortion (which explains the majority support for numerous restrictions on services) and, perhaps more important, in reframing abortion as an issue that supporters need to apologize for.

Similarly, within medicine, no evidence suggests that the larger antiabortion movement or the "prolife" caucuses of various medical groups have succeeded in making the majority of U.S. physicians opposed to legal abortion. What opponents of abortion *have* accomplished, however, is to convince the medical community of just how costly—in terms of time, energy and expenditure of political capital—incorporating abortion provision into mainstream medicine can be.

What, then, are the prospects for abortion provision in the United States in the next 30 years? Assuming that *Roe v. Wade* remains the law of the land, there are grounds for both considerable concern and cautious optimism. The opponents of abortion are not going away, and battles will continue to be waged on many fronts—vociferously in the halls of Congress and in front of clinics, and more quietly in hospital administrators' suites (as decisions are made about incorporating abortion services) and in offices of the small businesses (such as laundries) that are pressured by antiabortion groups not to service local clinics.

Prochoice forces will win some of these battles and lose others. Certainly, new technologies that have the potential to expand abortion access and to facilitate earlier abortions (and thus, perhaps, change the cultural meaning of abortion) are an important development, as are the numerous activities of newly energized prochoice medical organizations. Ultimately, however, the prochoice movement's greatest asset in this ongoing struggle is the extraordinary dedication of the health care professionals who have—in spite of everything—taken on abortion provision and developed a passion for their work that one rarely hears about in other areas of medicine.

*"Exposing the insincerities and confu-
sions in the rhetoric of 'life' and
'motherhood' in the abortion debate
frees up the debate from a vague, yet
often unquestioned, tie to embryonic or
fetal personhood."*

The Problem of Personhood in *Roe v. Wade*

Caitlin E. Borgmann

*Caitlin E. Borgmann, an associate professor at City University of
New York School of Law, was the state strategies coordinator at
the Reproductive Freedom Project of the American Civil Liberties
Union for six years. She has written widely about reproductive
rights and given testimony before several state legislatures on this
issue and is the editor of the Reproductive Rights Prof Blog.*

*In the following viewpoint, Borgmann analyzes the rhetoric
used in the abortion debate. She argues that conservative appeals
to "human life" are vague and deceptive, since most conservatives would not consistently treat a fetus as a legal person. Alter-
natively, liberals sidestep the question of fetal personhood, contending that principles of individual autonomy do not permit
any single view to be imposed upon everyone. Standard liberal
responses neglect the important role women's autonomy and dignity should play in the debate. Borgmann suggests that the question of embryonic or fetal personhood is misleading and distracts
from an honest public conversation about the morality of abortion.*

Caitlin E. Borgmann, "The Meaning of 'Life': Belief and Reason in the Abortion Debate," *ExpressO*, 2008. Reproduced by permission of the author.

The conservative portrayal of fetuses as persons pervades public discourse about abortion. For example, conservatives typically refer to a fetus or even an embryo as the "unborn *child*," suggesting that the fetus or embryo is equivalent to a baby or child and is distinguished solely by the happenstance of its physical or temporal location. . . . Within the abortion context, trial court judges have sometimes appointed a guardian *ad litem* to represent the embryo or fetus in judicial proceedings in which minors are seeking court permission for a confidential abortion. States have passed laws that require abortion providers to anesthetize the fetus before an abortion if the woman consents. Doctors who provide abortions have been sued for malpractice for failing to tell the woman that her embryo is "a complete, separate, and unique human being" . . .

Conservatives Imply That the Fetus Is a Person

The term "life," and its variants "human life" or "human being," are slippery terms, and conservatives have skillfully exploited their ambiguities to suggest that the embryo or fetus is a person without fully committing to this view. Justice [Anthony] Kennedy used this kind of rhetoric to bolster his ruling upholding the federal abortion ban in *Carhart II*. In a particularly controversial part of the opinion, Justice Kennedy wrote,

> Respect for human life finds an ultimate expression in the bond of love a mother has for her child. . . . Whether to have an abortion requires a difficult and painful moral decision. . . . [I]t seems unexceptionable to conclude some women come to regret their choice to abort the infant life they once created and sustained. . . . It is self-evident that a mother who comes to regret her choice to abort must struggle with grief more anguished and sorrow more profound when she learns . . . that she allowed a doctor to

pierce the skull and vacuum the fast-developing brain of her unborn child, a child assuming the human form.

The Court upheld the federal ban in part because it claimed that the Act prohibited a single procedure and could be safely circumvented by doctors providing abortions after the first trimester of pregnancy. Thus, Justice Kennedy clearly did not intend to say that a woman was committing murder in having an abortion. In fact, he seemed possibly to suggest that an embryo's moral status grows as it develops physically. But the words "infant life," "human life," "child," and "unborn child" call to mind, not embryos or fetuses, but babies. Kennedy's persistent references to the pregnant woman as a "mother" reinforce this perception. By invoking terms that suggest that abortion is murder, Kennedy appealed to a moral position that his own decision undermined: according to Kennedy, the Court's decision to uphold the ban would only steer physicians to other methods and would prevent not a single abortion from occurring.

Like Justice Kennedy, President [George W.] Bush discussed the federal ban in terms that evoked fetal personhood. In signing the ban, Bush asserted that "the most basic duty of government is to *defend the life* of the innocent. Every person, however frail or vulnerable, has *a place and a purpose in this world.*" His language was jarringly misplaced given the legislation's stated purpose, and instead seemed more appropriate for a total ban on abortions. . . .

Innocence and Guilt in Abortion Language

President Bush's use of the adjective, "innocent," only adds to the confusion. While "innocent" may mean "harmless," its more common meaning (and the one seemingly relevant here) is "free from sin or guilt" or "morally pure." "Innocence" in this sense is an attribute of personhood, since only persons are capable of being morally wrong. Bush's use of the term thus reinforces the impression that by "innocent human life" he means a person. But the use of "innocence" to describe the fetus is incongruous with the positions of many conservative politicians like Bush, who call for rape or incest exceptions to any ban on abortion. If embryos are "innocent," those that are the product of rape or incest are no less so. By insisting upon exceptions for rape or incest, conservatives instead seem more interested in the woman's perceived innocence (or guilt). A woman who is the victim of rape or incest is "innocent," in contrast with a woman who engages in consensual sex and who is considered morally culpable. In oral arguments in *Roe v. Wade*, Justice [Byron] White openly identified pregnant women as morally guilty. He asked counsel for Texas, Robert Flowers, "Well, if you're correct that the fetus is a person, then . . . the State would have great trouble permitting an abortion, would it?" Flowers answered that it would, unless the woman's life was at stake, in which case "there would be the balancing of the two lives." Justice White rejoined, "Well, what would you choose? Would you choose to kill the innocent one, or what?"

The impression that conservatives view most women who seek abortions as guilty and worthy of punishment is reinforced by a comprehensive study of the abortion and child welfare policies in the fifty states. One would expect that if abortion restrictions were really motivated by a belief in fetal or embryonic personhood, state laws restricting abortion would generally be accompanied by other child-protective laws. The study, however, showed the reverse. The states with the most restrictive abortion laws also spent the least to educate children, facilitate adoption, and provide assistance to poor children. The study's author found that this apparent contradiction was largely explained by hostility to women. The more hostile statewide public opinion was toward women's equality, and the lower women's income was relative to men's, the more likely a state was to restrict abortion. . . .

"Life" Means Different Things to Abortion Rights Advocates and Opponents

Because conservative politicians, political commentators, advocates, and scholars alike tend to use terms that evoke personhood in a confusing and often deceptive way, the discourse deserves careful examination. "Life" as employed by abortion rights opponents is a "thin" use of the word. To the extent it is rooted in fact, it refers to the fact that a blastocyst, or embryo, or fetus, is a human organism that is in the process of developing into a full person. Because abortion opponents want their view to be accepted as not necessarily tied to religious doctrine, they typically do not elaborate on the religious significance of this life, for example, that at a certain point it is ensouled. Their claim that the fetus is a "life" is thus a minimal assertion that does nothing to clarify the debate over abortion. There is no moral agency involved, nor even any awareness, at most stages of fetal development. Even doctors who provide abortions would not deny that a growing fetus is "living." And all would agree that the living fetus is of the human species.

This use of "life" stands in stark contrast to the life of a woman seeking an abortion, a woman whose own life is almost wholly disregarded in conservative rhetoric against abortion. Conservatives tend to ignore the "thick" conception of life that captures each particular pregnant woman's life in all its multi-layered complexity. [As Donald Dworkin writes in *Life's Dominion*:]

> Those who oppose abortion often use a process of visualization to stir people's emotions. Yet what they ask us to visualize is an isolated picture of a fetus. Where is the person who develops, nurtures, and sustains the fetus we are looking at? Where is the woman? In this vision, she is insignificant, devalued. When a woman does somehow momentarily enter our view, she is rendered translucent, a ghost of a real person.

A pregnant woman is situated in a time and place that is shaped by the narrative of her life and that is infused with moral obligations and aspirations, relationships, practical commitments, and religious and moral beliefs. She has experienced pleasure and pain, joy and sorrow, triumph and defeat. Along the way, events out of her control have shaped her life, but she has also helped to shape it. She may be a college student who is determined to pursue a particular career before or instead of becoming a mother. She may be a teenage victim of forcible incest who nonetheless managed to find her way to an abortion clinic. She may already be a mother of several children who knows that she cannot continue to provide a good life for her family if she bears another child. The conservative rhetoric wholly ignores—or, worse, trades upon—these deeper aspects of the term "life."

When conservatives concede the permissibility of a "life exception" for the woman in abortion regulations, they again ignore the complexity of real women's lives. What does it mean to save a woman's "life," in the context of an untenable pregnancy? In the nineteenth century, nearly all abortion prohibitions included a "therapeutic exception" allowing abortion when a physician determined it was necessary to preserve a woman's life. Most laws gave doctors unlimited discretion in deciding whether the exception was met. As Kristin Luker explains [in *Abortion and the Politics of Motherhood*], no laws defined precisely when a woman's "life" was at stake: "For example, must the threat be immediate or can it be long term? Similarly, they did not specify the confidence level needed. Must the pregnancy be an unquestionable threat to maternal life, or could the threat be only probable?" . . .

However, the contemporary conservative view of what it means to include a "life exception" for the woman has clearly narrowed. It no longer encompasses the kinds of social circumstances Luker describes. It does not include whether a pregnancy was caused by rape or incest. Nor does it include physical health risks to the woman that are short of life-endangering. Conservatives' diminished view of what a "life" exception means is evidenced by their adamant opposition to health exceptions in abortion legislation. In South Dakota, for example, a debate has raged over whether an abortion ban must include not only a life exception but one for rape, incest, and the woman's health.

Conservatives' use of the term "mother" is as thin as their references to "life." To the extent conservatives do look at the woman's life, they see her only as either embracing or rejecting motherhood. They view it as women's natural calling to be mothers. An anti-abortion-rights strategy memo proclaims that "abortion destroys the most important liberty interests women have in life." Of course, for women who do not feel a maternal impulse to the embryo or fetus or who have no desire to be mothers, now or ever, this label is falsely applied. Even for women to whom the concept of motherhood is applicable in some way, the conservative conception of "motherhood" is an impoverished one, for it looks only at the narrow snapshot of a pregnant woman and her fetus up to the point of birth. Abortion is portrayed as posing a binary set of choices: either the woman ends the pregnancy and rejects motherhood or she carries to term and embraces it.

Justice Kennedy, for example, suggested in *Carhart II*, that the question for all women facing unintended pregnancy is whether to heed the ultimate calling to be mothers or whether to do violence to that calling (at great risk to their mental stability). However, far from giving regard to a pregnant woman's life, such a romantic, idealized characterization of pregnant women as mothers snatches away the full picture of each particular woman's life and replaces it with an artificial and one-dimensional construct. The real complexities of motherhood are obviously not captured by this binary approach. It ignores the lifelong, irrevocable effect that motherhood has on a woman's future. It ignores the fact that the woman may already be a mother to existing children. It ignores the young woman who plans to be a mother in the future and knows that she must complete her education and grow more mature before she can be the kind of mother she aspires to be. It ignores the woman who cannot bear the thought of carrying and giving birth to her own child if she is unable to parent it.

Conflicting Meanings of Motherhood

Just how thin the conservative concept of motherhood is becomes apparent when one remembers that—if a pregnant woman or girl determines she is not fit or prepared to be a mother—conservatives blithely suggest that she should give birth anyway and give up her baby for adoption. What happens to the "bond of love" a woman supposedly has to the "infant life she once created and sustained" when she must relinquish her child? Why does it not seem "unexceptionable to conclude [that] some women come to regret their choice" to bear a child they cannot raise? Indeed, conservatives' disingenuous, thin invocation of motherhood sets women up for a lifetime of guilt when, having surrendered their babies for adoption, they later realize they have violated our culture's entrenched "ideal form of motherhood in which maternal presence has become the essence of good mothering." . . .

"So," one might respond to all this, "there are thick and thin conceptions of the terms 'life' and 'motherhood.' Why is it so objectionable for conservatives to use the thin conceptions of these terms?" The answer is that conservatives exploit the widely held *thick* conceptions of these terms in order to claim the moral high ground and gain sympathy in the abortion debate, even as they can only commit to the *thin* versions. They thus employ a kind of bait and switch: they know that when they invoke the words "life" and "mother," they instinctively conjure up for people the richer conceptions of these terms. To promote life in its thick sense carries a moral urgency and legitimacy. To be for motherhood in its thick sense is morally praiseworthy. When conservatives misleadingly use the term "life" in this way, they betray our trust. . . .

Conservatives would like to have us believe that to forbid abortions will lead to a greater appreciation of babies, children, and family relationships. But their political positions do nothing to further the thick conceptions of life that they invoke. We have reason to be concerned about many of the "life constraints" that shape not only women's decisions about abortion but also other important decisions such as whether to accept a particular job or to get married. . . .

The Abortion Debate Should Be Removed from Questions of Embryonic Personhood

Exposing the insincerities and confusions in the rhetoric of "life" and "motherhood" in the abortion debate frees up the debate from a vague, yet often unquestioned, tie to embryonic or fetal personhood. It helps to clear up what is—and is not—at stake when the state outlaws or regulates abortion. A conservative who does not in fact consistently view the embryo or fetus as a rights-holding person must justify why particular exceptions and not others are permissible, for example. This is not to say that a conservative might not still strongly believe abortion should be banned. But, if that conservative also asserts that there should be rape and incest exceptions, she will have to justify the inclusion of these particular exceptions without a generalized appeal to the need to protect "human life."

Perhaps the conservative will claim that pregnancies caused by rape and incest are particularly traumatic for the woman, and that in such cases the state's interest in developing human life does not outweigh the woman's interest in ridding herself of the traumatic pregnancy. This claim must then be measured against the many other traumatic circumstances in which women seeking abortions may find themselves. For example, are exceptions solely for life, rape, and incest fair if they exclude a woman carrying a much-wanted pregnancy who suddenly discovers that her fetus has a fatal anomaly, such as Tay-Sachs disease? What if a single mother of two learns that carrying her pregnancy to term will render her blind? What of a woman who suffers from schizophrenia or severe depression? The conservative view of abortion aims to have the law embody a particular moral view about abortion. But, because the conservative position lies on one extreme of the spectrum, and because the law must draw clear lines, the conservative approach cannot take account of the moral complexities of women's lives and the realities of the public's perception of the fetus's moral status.

Although conservative voters often profess support for laws limiting the availability of non-life-saving abortions to cases of rape and incest, one state's experience casts doubt on the likelihood that voters would ultimately accept such laws. In 2006, the South Dakota legislature enacted a ban on abortions that included only a narrowly drawn exception for women who would die if denied an abortion. When this ban was presented to voters through a ballot initiative, the measure was defeated. Opinion polls suggested that voters found the ban too extreme because it lacked exceptions for rape, incest, and the woman's health. Such exceptions were added in a second attempt to pass a ban in 2008, but voters again decisively rejected the measure. It seemed that once the exceptions were codified, voters lost their stomach for the ban altogether. The South Dakota experience demonstrates the difficulty of settling upon certain limited situations that merit abortions, defining those contexts with particularity, and determining the appropriate penalty. The public may seem comfortable in the abstract with laws that dictate the circumstances under which women may have abortions, but when it comes to drafting actual legislative intervention, the endeavor becomes unacceptably difficult and distasteful.

The liberal view of abortion, on the other hand, carries its own difficulties. In contrast with the conservative view, the liberal approach tends to treat the moral complexities of the abortion issue as operating in a sphere wholly separate from the law regulating abortion. Consequently, its defense of the right is unnecessarily weak. It gives a free pass to conservatives who speak ringingly of life and motherhood, but whose positions do not live up to their rhetoric. Moreover, it invites criticisms of the right to abortion as a right borne of selfishness and moral bankruptcy. While the conservative position simplifies discussions of abortion into ultimately untenable, black-and-white platitudes about "life" and "motherhood," liberals' unwillingness to engage in a discussion of the moral dimensions of the embryo or fetus strikes many abortion opponents as dismissive. . . .

Liberals Should Acknowledge the Moral Significance of Abortion

Liberals, like conservatives, need to appeal to public reason on abortion. This means acknowledging the moral significance of the abortion decision, rather than professing agnosticism. The view that seems most consistent with other considered ethical norms is a gradualist view of human life. At its earliest stages, human life is morally significant, but not sufficiently so to outweigh other important moral interests. This explains our wariness over embryonic stem cell research, yet accommodates the common view that such research is permissible when aimed at alleviating human suffering and curing disease. It also explains our acceptance of the creation of embryos, most of which will never be used, in order to allow couples to reproduce when it would otherwise not be possible. And it explains why early miscarriages, while no doubt often traumatic, are not viewed as the equivalent of losing a child (no funeral is held, for example). Fetuses late in pregnancy are viewed with far greater moral regard than embryos, but even in these circumstances the most ardent abortion opponents believe the woman's life takes precedence.

To view human life as intrinsically valuable does not mean abortion must be prohibited, however. The question remains how to weigh human life that has not yet reached the moral status of a person against a woman's interest in ending an unwanted or untenable pregnancy. Abortion is one of many morally significant decisions that adults make throughout their lives. These decisions may implicate the wellbeing, and even the life or death, of others. Parents leave children out of their wills. Children neglect to care for aging parents. A sister refuses to donate blood to her brother, although both share a rare blood type. While some of these decisions may seem selfish and morally indefensible, we do not presume that the state is in a better position to make them. We understand that these kinds of moral decisions are too complex and nuanced for the law to address. We accept that moral autonomy comes at the cost of occasional moral missteps.

Abortion is no different. Unintended pregnancy poses a nuanced moral question that the law is simply too crude and clumsy to answer. A woman's interest in ending an unwanted pregnancy weighs heavily on the other side of the balance. Her interest may well be influenced by moral concerns that most would agree justify ending her pregnancy, such as regard for her existing children, the desire to preserve her own health, or the hope of finishing school in order to escape a life of poverty. Her bodily integrity is also at stake. Some say that to force unwanted pregnancy upon any woman, regardless of her circumstances, is a moral harm far worse than the destruction of an embryo or fetus, while others vigorously disagree. . . .

It is likely that the law can never sufficiently capture the thick conceptions of life and motherhood in order to dictate whether a particular abortion is morally permissible. Even if it could, it is not clear that we should use the law in this way. While the law may set a floor for minimally moral conduct, to transform every moral aspiration into a legal command takes moral decisions out of individuals' hands in a way that denies them their moral agency. As [Laurence] Tribe says [in *Abortion: The Clash of Absolutes*], "to impose virtue on any person demeans that person's individual worth." If a woman declines an abortion only because the law tells her to do so, there is nothing to admire or condemn. We trust men and women to make profoundly moral decisions every day. Abortion should be no exception.

To view abortion as a morally weighty decision that women are empowered to make and that should be constitutionally protected is as consistent with the modern notion of "privacy," which speaks to individual autonomy, as it is with an alternative view of abortion rights as grounded in women's equality. But, rather than continuing to sidestep the moral discussion about abortion as though it has nothing to add to the constitutional discussion, evolving conceptions of the right to abortion should incorporate a greater attention to and awareness of the moral dimensions of the right, and should recognize women as moral agents empowered to endeavor to make the best decision for themselves and their families.

CHAPTER 2

Requiring Parental Notification for Minors Seeking Abortion

Case Overview

Ohio v. Akron Center for Reproductive Health (1990)

Ohio v. Akron Center for Reproductive Health is representative of several Supreme Court cases in the 1980s and 1990s involving parental notification and consent laws for minors seeking an abortion. *Ohio v. Akron Center for Reproductive Health* concerned an Ohio bill (Amended Substitute House Bill 319, or H.B. 319) that made it a crime for a physician to perform an abortion on an unemancipated minor without providing timely notice to one of the minor's parents. It mandated that at least twenty-four hours before performing an abortion on an unemancipated minor, a physician must notify a parent, or, if the minor fears emotional or other abuse from her parents, an adult brother, sister, step-parent, or grandparent. If the minor is unwilling to notify a parent or specified parent-substitute, she may go to juvenile court and obtain a judicial bypass order, or an order authorizing that the minor need not obtain consent, by presenting "clear and convincing evidence" that she has sufficient maturity and information to make the abortion decision herself, that one of her parents has engaged in a pattern of physical, emotional, or sexual abuse, or that giving such notice is otherwise not in her best interests. Shortly before H.B. 319's effective date, an abortion facility, a physician who worked at the facility, and a pregnant minor, among others, challenged the statute's constitutionality in the district court, which ultimately issued an injunction preventing H.B. 319's enforcement. The Sixth Circuit Court of Appeals found that several of the statute's provisions were unconstitutional.

The Supreme Court disagreed, ruling 6-3 that a state law requiring notice to one parent with a judicial bypass does not place an undue burden on a minor and is therefore constitutional. In the Court's majority opinion, Anthony Kennedy wrote:

> The State is entitled to assume that, for most of its people, the beginnings of that understanding will be within the family, society's most intimate association. It is both rational and fair for the State to conclude that, in most instances, the family will strive to give a lonely or even terrified minor advice that is both compassionate and mature.

In his dissent, Harry Blackmun expressed concern for minors who were abused or neglected, saying: "A minor needs no statute to seek the support of loving parents. Where trust and confidence exist within the family structure, it is likely that communication already exists. If that compassionate support is lacking, an unwanted pregnancy is a poor way to generate it."

The constitutionality of parental notification and consent was first decided in *Bellotti v. Baird* (1979) and reaffirmed in *Planned Parenthood of Kansas City v. Ashcroft* (1983), *Hodgson v. Minnesota* (1989), and *Ohio v. Akron Center for Reproductive Health* (1990). According to the National Abortion Federation, forty-four states have passed laws requiring either parental notification or parental consent for a minor seeking an abortion.

> *"It would deny all dignity to the family to say that the State cannot ... regulat[e] its health professions to ensure that, in most cases, a young woman will receive guidance and understanding from a parent."*

Majority Opinion: State Laws May Require Parental Notification for Minors Seeking Abortion

Anthony Kennedy

Anthony Kennedy was appointed to the Supreme Court in 1988 by President Ronald Reagan after the Senate rejected Reagan's first nominee, Robert Bork. A generally conservative justice, Kennedy supports a broad reading of the "liberty" protected by the Due Process Clause of the Fourteenth Amendment, which means he supports a constitutional right to abortion in principle, though he has voted to uphold several restrictions on that right, including laws to prohibit partial-birth abortions.

Writing for the 6-3 majority in Ohio v. Akron Center *(1990), Kennedy determines that an Ohio statute that prohibits any person from performing an abortion on an unmarried, unemancipated, minor female without notice to one of the parents or a court order or approval is constitutional. He argues that the burden of proof required by the minor is permissible, that the amount of time required to follow procedure is appropriate, and that the procedures are not unduly confusing.*

Anthony Kennedy, majority opinion, *Ohio v. Akron Center*, U.S. Supreme Court, June 25, 1990.

The Court of Appeals held invalid an Ohio statute that, with certain exceptions, prohibits any person from performing an abortion on an unmarried, unemancipated, minor woman absent notice to one of the woman's parents or a court order of approval. We reverse, for we determine that the statute accords with our precedents on parental notice and consent in the abortion context, and does not violate the Fourteenth Amendment.

The Ohio Legislature, in November 1985, enacted Amended Substitute House Bill 319 (H.B. 319), . . . [T]he cornerstone of this legislation, makes it a criminal offense, except in four specified circumstances, for a physician or other person to perform an abortion on an unmarried and unemancipated woman under eighteen years of age.

The first and second circumstances in which a physician may perform an abortion relate to parental notice and consent. First, a physician may perform an abortion if he provides "at least twenty-four hours actual notice, in person or by telephone," to one of the women's parents (or her guardian or custodian) of his intention to perform the abortion. The physician, as an alternative, may notify a minor's adult brother, sister, stepparent, or grandparent, if the minor and the other relative each file an affidavit in the juvenile court stating that the minor fears physical, sexual, or severe emotional abuse from one of her parents. If the physician cannot give the notice "after a reasonable effort," he may perform the abortion after "at least forty-eight hours constructive notice" by both ordinary and certified mail. Second, a physician may perform an abortion on the minor if one of her parents (or her guardian or custodian) has consented to the abortion in writing.

The Judicial Bypass Procedure

The third and fourth circumstances depend on a judicial procedure that allows a minor to bypass the notice and consent provisions just described. The statute allows a physician to perform an abortion without notifying one of the minor's parents or receiving the parent's consent if a juvenile court issues an order authorizing the minor to consent, or if a juvenile court or court of appeals, by its inaction, provides constructive authorization for the minor to consent.

The bypass procedure requires the minor to file a complaint in the juvenile court, stating (1) that she is pregnant; (2) that she is unmarried, under 18 years of age, and unemancipated; (3) that she desires to have an abortion without notifying one of her parents; (4) that she has sufficient maturity and information to make an intelligent decision whether to have an abortion without such notice, or that one of her parents has engaged in a pattern of physical, sexual, or emotional abuse against her, or that notice is not in her best interests; and (5) that she has or has not retained an attorney. . . .

The juvenile court must hold a hearing at the earliest possible time, but not later than the fifth business day after the minor files the complaint. The court must render its decision immediately after the conclusion of the hearing. Failure to hold the hearing within this time results in constructive authorization for the minor to consent to the abortion. At the hearing, the court must appoint a guardian ad litem and an attorney to represent the minor if she has not retained her own counsel. The minor must prove her allegation of maturity, pattern of abuse, or best interests by clear and convincing evidence, and the juvenile court must conduct the hearing to preserve the anonymity of the complainant, keeping all papers confidential.

The minor has the right to expedited review. The statute provides that, within four days after the minor files a, notice of appeal, the clerk of the juvenile court shall deliver the notice of appeal and record to the state court of appeals. The clerk of the court of appeals dockets the appeal upon receipt of these items. The minor must file her brief within four days after the docketing. If she desires an oral argument, the court of appeals must hold one within five days after the docketing and must issue a decision immediately after oral argument. If she waives the right to an oral argument, the court of appeals must issue a decision within five days after the docketing. If the court of appeals does not comply with these time limits, a constructive order results authorizing the minor to consent to the abortion. . . .

The Importance of Precedent

We have decided five cases addressing the constitutionality of parental notice or parental consent statutes in the abortion context. See *Planned Parenthood of Central Mo. v. Danforth*, (1976); *Bellotti v. Baird*, (1979); *H.L. v. Matheson*, (1981); *Planned Parenthood Assn. of Kansas City, Mo., Inc. v. Ashcroft*, (1983); *Akron v. Akron Center for Reproductive Health, Inc.*, (1983). We do not need to determine whether a statute that does not accord with these cases would violate the Constitution, for we conclude that H.B. 319 is consistent with them.

This dispute turns, to a large extent, on the adequacy of H.B. 319's judicial bypass procedure. In analyzing this aspect of the dispute, we note that, although our cases have required bypass procedures for parental consent statutes, we have not decided whether parental notice statutes must contain such procedures. We leave the question open, because, whether or not the Fourteenth Amendment requires notice statutes to contain bypass procedures, H.B. 319's bypass procedure meets the requirements identified for parental consent statutes in *Danforth, Bellotti, Ashcroft,* and *Akron. Danforth* established that, in order to prevent another person from having an absolute veto power over a minor's decision to have an abortion, a State must provide some sort of bypass procedure if it elects to require parental consent. . . . [I]t is a corollary to the greater intrusiveness of consent statutes that a bypass procedure that will suffice for a consent statute will suffice also for a notice statute.

The principal opinion in *Bellotti* stated four criteria that a bypass procedure in a consent statute must satisfy. Appellees contend that the bypass procedure does not satisfy these criteria. We disagree. First, the Bellotti principal opinion indicated that the procedure must allow the minor to show that she possesses the maturity and information to make her abortion decision, in consultation with her physician, without regard to her parents' wishes. The Court reaffirmed this requirement in Akron by holding that a State cannot presume the immaturity of girls under the age of 15. In the case now before us, we have no difficulty concluding that H.B. 319 allows a minor to show maturity in conformity with the principal opinion in Bellotti. The statute permits the minor to show that she "is sufficiently mature and well enough informed to decide intelligently whether to have an abortion."

Second, the *Bellotti* principal opinion indicated that the procedure must allow the minor to show that, even if she cannot make the abortion decision by herself, "the desired abortion would be in her best interests." We believe that H.B. 319 satisfies the *Bellotti* language as quoted. The statute requires the juvenile court to authorize the minor's consent where the court determines that the abortion is in the minor's best interest and in cases where the minor has shown a pattern of physical, sexual, or emotional abuse.

Third, the *Bellotti* principal opinion indicated that the procedure must insure the minor's anonymity. H.B. 319 satisfies this standard. Section 2151.85(D) provides that "[t]he [juvenile] court shall not notify the parents, guardian, or custodian of the complainant that she is pregnant or that she wants to have an abortion." . . .

Anonymity Not Required

Confidentiality differs from anonymity, but we do not believe that the distinction has constitutional significance in the present context. The distinction has not played a part in our previous decisions, and, even if the Bellotti principal opinion is taken as setting the standard, we do not find complete anonymity critical. H.B. 319, like the statutes in *Bellotti* and *Ashcroft*, takes reasonable steps to prevent the public from learning of the minor's identity. We refuse to base a decision on the facial validity of a statute on the mere possibility of unauthorized, illegal disclosure by state employees. H.B. 319, like many sophisticated judicial procedures, requires participants to provide identifying information for administrative purposes, not for public disclosure.

Fourth, the *Bellotti* plurality indicated that courts must conduct a bypass procedure with expedition to allow the minor an effective opportunity to obtain the abortion. H.B. 319, as noted above, requires the trial court to make its decision within five "business day[s]" after the minor files her complaint, requires the court of appeals to docket an appeal within four "days" after the minor files a notice of appeal; and requires the court of appeals to render a decision within five "days" after docketing the appeal, ibid.

The District Court and the Court of Appeals assumed that all of the references to days in 2151.85(B)(1) and 2505.073(A) meant business days, as opposed to calendar days. They calculated, as a result, that the procedure could take up to 22 calendar days, because the minor could file at a time during the year in which the 14 business days needed for the bypass procedure would encompass three Saturdays, three Sundays, and two legal holidays. Appellees maintain, on the basis of an affidavit included in the record, that a 3-week delay could increase by a substantial measure both the costs and the medical risks of an abortion. They conclude, as did those courts, that H.B. 319 does not satisfy the *Bellotti* principal opinion's expedition requirement.

As a preliminary matter, the 22-day calculation conflicts with two well-known rules of construction discussed in our abortion cases and elsewhere. . . . Although we recognized that the other federal courts "'are better schooled in and more able to interpret the laws of their respective States'" than we we, the Court of Appeals' decision strikes us as dubious. Interpreting the term "days" in 2505.073(A) to mean business days instead of calendar days seems inappropriate and unnecessary because of the express and contrasting use of "business day[s]" in 2151.85(B)(1). In addition, because appellees are making a facial challenge to a statute, they must show that "no set of circumstances exists under which the Act would be valid." The Court of Appeals should not have invalidated the Ohio statute on a facial challenge based upon a worst-case analysis that may never occur. Moreover, under our precedents, the mere possibility that the procedure may require up to 22 days in a rare case is plainly insufficient to invalidate the statute on its face. *Ashcroft*, for example, upheld a Missouri statute that contained a bypass procedure that could require 17 calendar days plus a sufficient time for deliberation and decisionmaking at both the trial and appellate levels. . . .

Minors Can Demonstrate Maturity

We discern no constitutional defect in the statute. Absent a demonstrated pattern of abuse or defiance, a State may expect that its judges will follow mandated procedural requirements. There is no showing that the time limitation imposed by H.B. 319 will be ignored. With an abundance of caution, and concern for the minor's interests, Ohio added the constructive authorization provision in H.B. 319 to ensure expedition of the bypass procedures even if these time limits are not met. The State Attorney General represents that a physician can obtain certified documentation from the juvenile or appellate court that constructive authorization has occurred. We did not require a similar safety net in the bypass procedures in *Ashcroft*, and find no defect in the procedures that Ohio has provided.

Second, appellees ask us to rule that a bypass procedure cannot require a minor to prove maturity or best interests by a standard of clear and convincing evidence. They maintain that when a State seeks to deprive an individual of liberty interests, it must take upon itself the risk of error. House Bill 319 violates this standard, in their opinion, not only by placing the burden of proof upon the minor, but also by imposing a heightened standard of proof.

This contention lacks merit. A State does not have to bear the burden of proof on the issues of maturity or best interests. . . .

Third, appellees contend that the pleading requirements in H.B. 319 create a trap for the unwary. The minor, under the statutory scheme and the requirements prescribed by the Ohio Supreme Court, must choose among three pleading forms. The first alleges only maturity and time second alleges only best interests. She may not attempt to prove both maturity and best interests unless she chooses the third form, which alleges both of these facts. Appellees contend that the complications imposed by this scheme deny a minor the opportunity, required by the principal opinion in *Bellotti*, to prove either maturity or best interests or both.

Even on the assumption that the pleading scheme could produce some initial confusion because few minors would have counsel when pleading, the simple and straightforward procedure does not deprive the minor of an opportunity to prove her case. It seems unlikely that the Ohio courts will treat a minors choice of complaint form without due care and understanding for her unrepresented status. In addition, we note that the minor does not make a binding election by the initial choice of pleading form. The minor, under H.B. 319, receives appointed counsel after filing the complaint and may move for leave to amend the pleadings.

Physician May Notify Parents

Appellees, as a final matter, contend that we should invalidate H.B. 319 in its entirety because the statute requires the parental notice to be given by the physician who is to perform the abortion. In *Akron*, the Court found unconstitutional a requirement that the attending physician provide the information and counseling relevant to informed consent. Although the Court did not disapprove of informing a woman of the health risks of an abortion, it explained that "[t]he State's interest is in ensuring that the woman's consent is informed and unpressured; the critical factor is whether she obtains the necessary information and counseling from a qualified person, not the identity of the person from whom she obtains it." Appellees maintain, in a similar fashion, that Ohio has no reason for requiring the minor's physician, rather than some other qualified person, to notify one of the minor's parents.

Appellees, however, have failed to consider our precedent on this matter. We upheld, in *Matheson*, a statute that required a physician to notify the minor's parents. The distinction between notifying a minor's parents and informing a woman of the routine risks of an abortion has ample justification; although counselors may provide information about general risks as in *Akron*, appellees do not contest the superior ability of a physician to garner and use information supplied by a minor's parents upon receiving notice. We continue to believe that a State may require the physician himself or herself to take reasonable steps to notify a minor's parent, because the parent often will provide important medical data to the physician. As we explained in *Matheson*:

> "The medical, emotional, and psychological consequences of an abortion are serious, and can be lasting; this is particularly so when the patient is immature. An adequate medical and psychological cast history is important to the physician. Parents can provide medical and psychological data, refer the physician to other sources of medical history, such as family physicians, and authorize family physicians to give relevant data."

The conversation with the physician, in addition, may enable a parent to provide better advice to the minor. The parent who must respond to an event with complex philosophical and emotional dimensions is given some access to an experienced and, in an ideal case, detached physician who can assist the parent in approaching the problem in a mature and balanced way. This access may benefit both the parent and child in a manner not possible through notice by less qualified persons. . . .

The Ohio statute, in sum, does not impose an undue, or otherwise unconstitutional, burden on a minor seeking an abortion. We believe, in addition, that the legislature acted in a rational manner in enacting H.B. 319. A free and enlightened society may decide that each of its members should attain a clearer, more tolerant understanding of the profound philosophic choices confronted by a woman who is considering whether to seek an abortion. Her decision will embrace her own destiny and personal dignity, and the origins of the other human life that lie within the embryo. The State is entitled to assume that, for most of its people, the beginnings of that understanding will be within the family, society's most intimate association. It is both rational and fair for the State to conclude that, in most instances, the family will strive to give a lonely or even terrified minor advice that is both compassionate and mature. The statute in issue here is a rational way to further those ends. It would deny all dignity to the family to say that the State cannot take this reasonable step in regulating its health professions to ensure that, in most cases, a young woman will receive guidance and understanding from a parent. We uphold H.B. 319 on its face, and reverse the Court of Appeals.

It is so ordered.

| "Rather than create a judicial bypass system that reflects the sensitivity necessary when dealing with a minor making this deeply intimate decision, Ohio has created a tortuous maze."

Dissenting Opinion: Parental Notification Laws Are an Unjustified Intrusion into a Private Decision

Harry Blackmun

Harry Blackmun (1908–1999) served on the Supreme Court from 1970 until 1994. Although he was a lifelong Republican appointed to the Supreme Court by President Richard Nixon, Blackmun soon emerged as a sympathetic liberal. He wrote the majority opinion in Roe v. Wade *(1973), which recognized a woman's constitutional right to abortion.*

In his dissenting opinion in Ohio v. Akron Center *(1990), Justice Blackmun argues that the parental notification process outlined in the statute creates unnecessary obstacles for a minor seeking an abortion; of particular concern is the effect of the law on minors who are sexually or physically abused by their parents.*

The State of Ohio has acted with particular insensitivity in enacting the statute the Court today upholds. Rather than create a judicial bypass system that reflects the sensitivity necessary when dealing with a minor making this deeply intimate

Harry Blackmun, dissenting opinion, *Ohio v. Akron Center*, U.S. Supreme Court, June 25, 1990.

decision, *Ohio* has created a tortuous maze. Moreover, the State has failed utterly to show that it has any significant state interest in deliberately placing its pattern of obstacles in the path of the pregnant minor seeking to exercise her constitutional right to terminate a pregnancy. The challenged provisions of the Ohio statute are merely "poorly disguised elements of discouragement for the abortion decision." . . .

The obstacle course begins when the minor first enters the courthouse to fill out the complaint forms. The "pleading trap," requires the minor to choose among three forms. The first alleges only maturity; the second alleges only that the abortion is in her best interest. Only if the minor chooses the third form, which alleges both, may the minor attempt to prove both maturity and best interest as is her right under *Bellotti II* [*Bellotti v. Baird* (1979)]. The majority makes light of what it acknowledges might be "some initial confusion" of the unsophisticated minor who is trying to deal with an unfamiliar and mystifying court system on an intensely intimate matter. The Court points out that the minor, with counsel appointed after she files the complaint, "may move for leave to amend the pleadings" and avers that it "seems unlikely that the Ohio courts will treat a minor's choice of complaint form without due care." I would take the Ohio Legislature's word, however, that its pleading requirement was intended to be meaningful. The constitutionality of a procedural provision cannot be analyzed on the basis that it may have no effect. If the pleading requirement prevents some minors from showing either that they are mature or that an abortion would be in their best interests, it plainly is unconstitutional. . . .

An Obstacle Course

As the pregnant minor attempts to find her way through the labyrinth set up by the State of Ohio, she encounters yet another obstruction even before she has completed the complaint form. In *Bellotti II* the plurality insisted that the judicial bypass procedure "must assure that a resolution of the issue, and any appeals that may follow, will be completed with anonymity . . ." That statement was not some idle procedural requirement, but stems from the proposition that the Due Process Clause protects the woman's right to make her decision "independently and privately." The zone of privacy long has been held to encompass an "individual interest in avoiding disclosure of personal matters." The Ohio statute does not safeguard that right. Far from keeping the identity of the minor anonymous, the statute requires the minor to sign her full name and the name of one of her parents on the complaint form. Acknowledging that "[c]onfidentiality differs from anonymity," the majority simply asserts that "complete anonymity" is not "critical." That easy conclusion is irreconcilable with *Bellotti's* anonymity requirement. The definition of "anonymous" is "not named or identified." Complete anonymity, then, appears to be the only kind of anonymity that a person could possibly have. The majority admits that case law regarding the anonymity requirement has permitted no less.

The majority points to Ohio laws requiring court employees not to disclose public documents, blithely assuming that the "mere possibility of unauthorized, illegal disclosure by state employees" is insufficient to establish that the confidentiality of the proceeding is not protected. In fact, the provisions regarding the duty of court employees not to disclose public documents amount to no more than "generally stated principles of . . . confidentiality." As the District Court pointed out, there are no indications of how a clerk's office, large or small, is to ensure that the records of abortion cases will be distinguished from the records of all other cases that are available to the public. Nor are there measures for sealing the record after the case is closed to prevent its public availability. This Court is well aware that, unless special care is taken, court documents of an intimate nature will find their way to the press and public. The State has offered no justification for its failure to provide specific guidelines to be followed by the Juvenile Court to ensure anonymity for the pregnant minor— even though it has in place a procedure to assure the anonymity of juveniles who have been adjudicated delinquent or unruly.

"A woman and her physician will necessarily be more reluctant to choose an abortion if there exists a possibility that her decision and her identity will become known publicly." A minor whose very purpose in going through a judicial bypass proceeding is to avoid notifying a hostile or abusive parent would be most alarmed at signing her name and the name of her parent on the complaint form. Generalized statements concerning the confidentiality of records would be of small comfort, even if she were aware of them. True anonymity is essential to an effective, meaningful bypass. In the face of the forms that the minor must actually deal with, the State's assurances that the minor's privacy will be protected ring very hollow. I would not permit the State of Ohio to force a minor to forgo her anonymity in order to obtain a waiver of the parental notification requirement.

Pregnant Teens Should Not Face Delay

Because a "pregnant adolescent . . . cannot preserve for long the possibility of aborting, which effectively expires in a matter of weeks from the onset of pregnancy," this Court has required that the State "must assure" that the resolution of the issue, and any appeals that may follow, will be completed with . . . sufficient expedition to provide an effective opportunity for an abortion to be obtained. Ohio's judicial bypass procedure can consume up to three weeks of a young woman's pregnancy. I would join the Sixth Circuit, the District Court, and the other federal courts that have held that a timespan of this length fails to guarantee a sufficiently expedited procedure.

The majority is unconcerned that "the procedure may require up to 22 days in a rare case." I doubt the "rarity" of such cases. In any event, the Court of Appeals appropriately pointed out that, because a minor often does not learn of her pregnancy until a late stage in the first trimester, time lost during that trimester is especially critical. The Court ignores the facts that the medical risks surrounding abortion increase as pregnancy advances, and that such delay may push a woman into her second trimester, where the medical risks, economic costs, and state regulation increase dramatically. Minors, who are more likely to seek later abortions than adult women, and who usually are not financially independent, will suffer acutely from any delay. Because a delay of up to 22 days may limit significantly a woman's ability to obtain an abortion, I agree with the conclusions of the District Court and the Court of Appeals that the statute violates this Court's command that a judicial bypass proceeding be conducted with sufficient speed to maintain "an effective opportunity for an abortion to be obtained."

The Ohio statute provides that, if the juvenile or appellate courts fail to act within the statutory timeframe, an abortion without parental notification is "constructively" authorized. Although Ohio's Legislature may have intended this provision to expedite the bypass procedure, the confusion that will result from the constructive authorization provision will add further delay to the judicial bypass proceeding, and is yet one more obstruction in the path of the pregnant minor. The physician risks civil damages, criminal penalties, including imprisonment, as well as revocation of his license for disobeying the statute's commands, but the statute provides for no formal court order or other relief to safeguard the physician from these penalties. The State argues that a combination of a date-stamped copy of the minor's complaint and a "docket sheet showing no entry" would inform the physician that the abortion could proceed. Yet the mere absence of an entry on a court's docket sheet hardly would be reassuring to a physician facing such dire consequences, and the State offers no reason why a formal order or some kind of actual notification from the clerk of court would not be possible. There is no doubt that the nebulous authorization envisioned by this statute "in conjunction with a statute imposing strict civil and criminal liability . . . could have a profound chilling effect on the will-ingness of physicians to perform abortions. . . ." I agree with the Court of Appeals that the "practical effect" of the "pocket approval" provision is to frustrate the minor's right to an ex-pedient disposition of her petition.

Judicial Bypass Process

If the minor is able to wend her way through the intricate course of preliminaries *Ohio* has set up for her and at last reaches the court proceeding, the State shackles her even more tightly with still another "extra layer and burden of regulation on the abortion decision." The minor must demonstrate by "clear and convincing evidence" either (1) her maturity; (2) or that one of her parents has engaged in a pattern of physical, sexual, or emotional abuse against her; or (3) that notice to a parent "is not in her best interest." The imposition of this heightened standard of proof unduly burdens the minor's right to seek an abortion and demonstrates a fundamental misunderstanding of the real nature of a court bypass pro-ceeding.

The function of a standard of proof is to "'instruct the factfinder concerning the degree of confidence our society thinks he should have in the correctness of factual conclusions,'" and is "a societal judgment about how the risk of error should be distributed between the litigants." By im-posing such a stringent standard of proof, this *Ohio* statute improperly places the risk of an erroneous decision on the minor, the very person whose fundamental right is at stake. Even if the judge is satisfied that the minor is mature or that an abortion is in her best interest, the court may not authorize the procedure unless it additionally finds that the evidence meets a "clear and convincing" standard of proof. . . .

Although I think the provision is constitutionally infirm for all minors, I am particularly concerned about the effect it will have on sexually or physically abused minors. I agree that parental interest in the welfare of their children is "particularly strong where a normal family relationship exists." A minor needs no statute to seek the support of loving parents. Where trust and confidence exist within the family structure, it is likely that communication already exists. If that compassionate support is lacking, an unwanted pregnancy is a poor way to generate it.

Sadly, not all children in our country are fortunate enough to be members of loving families. For too many young pregnant women, parental involvement in this most intimate decision threatens harm, rather than promises comfort.

The Court's selective blindness to this stark social reality is bewildering and distressing. Lacking the protection that young people typically find in their intimate family associations, these minors are desperately in need of constitutional protection. The sexually or physically abused minor may indeed be "lonely or even terrified," not of the abortion procedure, but of an abusive family member. The Court's placid reference, ibid., to the "compassionate and mature" advice the minor will receive from within the family must seem an unbelievable and cruel irony to those children trapped in violent families.

Under the system *Ohio* has set up, a sexually abused minor must go to court and demonstrate to a complete stranger by clear and convincing evidence that she has been the victim of a pattern of sexual abuse. When asked at argument what kind of evidence a minor would be required to adduce at her bypass hearing, the State answered that the minor would tell her side to the judge and the judge would consider how well "the minor is able to articulate what her particular concerns are." The court procedure alone, in many cases, is extremely traumatic. The State and the Court are impervious to the additional burden imposed on the abused minor who, as any experienced social worker or counselor knows, is often afraid and ashamed to reveal what has happened to her to anyone outside the home. The Ohio statute forces that minor, despite her very real fears, to experience yet one more hardship. She must attempt, in public, and before strangers, to "articulate what her particular concerns are" with sufficient clarity to meet the State's "clear and convincing evidence" standard. The upshot is that, for the abused minor, the risk of error entails a risk of violence.

I would affirm the judgments below on the grounds of the several constitutional defects identified by the District Court and the Court of Appeals. The pleading requirements, the so-called and fragile guarantee of anonymity, the insufficiency of the expedited procedures, the constructive authorization provision, and the "clear and convincing evidence" requirement, singly and collectively, cross the limit of constitutional acceptance.

> "Pro-choice and pro-life advocates . . .
> disagree sharply on whether [parental]
> involvement should be the choice of the
> young woman or mandated by law."

The Results of Parental Notification Laws Have Been Mixed

Kathleen Sylvester

Kathleen Sylvester is director of the Social Policy Action Network, a nonprofit organization that promotes effective social policy. An award-winning journalist, she is also the founder of and senior writer for Governing, *a national magazine of state and local public policy.*

In the following viewpoint, Sylvester notes that a majority of those who support abortion rights believe that parents should be informed when their pregnant minor is considering an abortion; however, such laws are difficult to enforce.

With increasing frequency, courts and legislatures are giving adolescents more latitude in making their own medical decisions. They are permitted by many states to consent to their own treatment—without parental permission—for drug abuse, mental illness or sexually transmitted diseases.

But when it comes to abortion, the trend is in the other direction—toward more parental involvement. And the intensity of the debate is making for a clear confrontation over when the state can interfere with the fundamental relationship between parent and child.

Whether minors should be able to obtain abortions without parental consent is not an issue that breaks along predictable lines. Indeed, a number of polls show that a majority of those who support abortion rights believe that parents should be informed when a daughter is considering such a procedure.

Disagreement on Parental Involvement

But although both pro-choice and pro-life advocates support the basic premise that no young woman considering an abortion should make such a difficult choice without parental involvement, their agreement stops there. They disagree sharply on whether that involvement should be the choice of the young woman or mandated by law.

And with more than 400,000 teenagers under the age of 18 becoming pregnant every year, and 180,000 choosing to have abortions, parental notification has become an issue of growing concern to state legislators. Both sides are making impassioned arguments in more than a dozen state legislatures, where bills requiring parental notification or consent before a minor has an abortion have been introduced this year [1993].

At least one of those bills—South Dakota's—was drafted with the intention of carving out a standard that will pass constitutional muster in the U.S. Supreme Court and become a national model. The bill, which was awaiting the governor's signature late last month [March 1993], would require physicians to notify one parent of a minor seeking an abortion. [The bill was signed into law in 1993.] The parent must be notified by telephone or certified mail, and physicians must then wait 48 hours unless the parent consents. The requirement may be waived if the minor's health is in imminent danger or she declares that she has been abused.

The South Dakota measure is only one version of parental involvement legislation being considered this year. There are at least 11 other states—Arizona, Delaware, Connecticut, Nevada, New Hampshire, New Jersey, New York, Oklahoma, Texas, Utah and Vermont—where the two sides are contending.

Mandating Family Communication

"The government," says Sara Pines of the National Abortion Rights Action League [NARAL], "can't mandate family communication where it does not exist." NARAL and other organizations that support abortion rights point to a 1991 study by the Alan Guttmacher Institute indicating that 61 percent of young women considering abortions chose to tell at least one parent. Among the young women who opted not to tell their parents, 30 percent expressed fear of violent retribution or being forced to leave home.

Pro-life activists counter by criticizing what they consider to be a hypocritical legal system that holds parents responsible for the health and welfare of their children until those children are legally considered adults (usually at age 18) but would allow those same children to have abortions without parental knowledge. Burke Balch, legislative director of the National Right to Life Committee, suggests that while a young woman's first reaction to an unplanned pregnancy may be fear of telling her parents, such fears may prove unfounded.

About three dozen states currently require either one or both parents to be informed or to give permission before a minor daughter has an abortion. The legal framework that has guided legislators drafting these laws comes from the 1978 U.S. Supreme Court decision in *Bellotti vs. Baird*. In that case, the justices ruled that parental consent or notification laws were legal as long as they were accompanied by judicial bypass provisions. These permit courts to grant exceptions if a judge decides that a young woman is mature enough, or that regardless of her maturity, an abortion would be in her best interest.

Mixed Results

Since these laws were implemented, reports about their impact have been mixed. A 1986 study of Massachusetts law requiring the consent of both parents or a waiver from a judge found it had little effect in reducing the number of abortions obtained by unmarried women under age 18, in part because they got abortions in nearby states without such restrictions. But a 1991 study of Minnesota's two-parent notification law showed a drop-off in the abortion rate for minors, with the study's author concluding that parental notification encouraged "pregnancy avoidance."

The 1992 Supreme Court's landmark abortion case, *Planned Parenthood of Southeastern Pennsylvania vs. Casey,* left the *Bellotti* framework intact. Still, that does not please either side. Neither supporters nor opponents of abortion believe that the judicial bypass is a satisfactory compromise on the issue of parental involvement. Pro-choice advocates cite examples of pro-life judges who routinely deny young women's requests to have abortions without telling their parents. Pro-life advocates tell how abortion rights advocates "shop" for judges who consistently grant permission for abortions.

And in practice, while many states have parental notification or consent laws on their books, a large proportion of those laws are not enforced. Pro-choice advocates have successfully challenged many in court. According to NARAL statistics, there are 12 states in which such statutes have been invalidated or enjoined by courts or by state attorneys general. Some were struck down because they didn't meet the Supreme Court's requirement for a judicial bypass; others were faulted for the way in which the bypass was implemented—

either failing to protect the minor's privacy or failing to process her abortion request expeditiously.

Legal and Legislative Confusion

The legal maneuvers, uneven enforcement and conflicting evidence have left parental consent and notification in a state of legal and legislative confusion. The National Right to Life Committee hopes to clarify the picture.

Legislative director Balch suggests that the one-parent notification measures with no judicial bypass provision, such as South Dakota's, are most likely to pass state legislatures. And counting votes on the U.S. Supreme Court, he says that seven of the court's nine sitting justices have indicated receptivity to such a requirement in earlier opinions.

In the meantime, the National Abortion Rights Action League is lobbying hard for the U.S. Congress to pass the Freedom of Choice Act, which would codify the basic principles of *Roe vs. Wade* and prohibit states from restricting abortions prior to fetal viability. But Marcy Wilder, a NARAL attorney points out that the legislation does not address the rights of minors. So while the focus of the debate about the rights of women to have abortions is on Congress, the rights of as many as 400,000 of those women still rest with the states.

*"For some minors, parental notification
or consent laws are not just an obstacle
... [they] severely restrict their access
to safe, legal abortions."*

Teens Are Adversely Affected by Parental Notification Laws

Le Anne Schreiber

*Journalist Le Anne Schreiber was ombudsman for the ESPN
sports network until March 2009 and is a former* New York
Times *sports editor. She is the author of a book titled* Mid-
stream *and continues to write for publications ranging from*
Glamour *to the* Yale Review.

*In the following viewpoint Schreiber describes the real-life
cases of pregnant teenagers seeking abortion in Minnesota, where
parental notification and consent is mandatory. She notes that
proponents of notification laws view the typical families of girls
as intact and supportive, whereas opponents consider the reality
of the girls coming from broken or dysfunctional families.*

Nationally, over 180,000 minors a year seek abortions, and
about half of them voluntarily discuss the decision with
at least one parent. The other half have many reasons for not
confiding in their parents. A parent may be abusive, violent,
unknown to his/her daughter, emotionally or geographically
distant, staunchly antiabortion or too ill to receive distressing
news. Some young women are fearful that the news will disap-
point their parents intensely. As Natalie Davidson, who went

to court in Duluth [Minnesota] rather than notify a father she had never met, put it, "This law really makes me mad, because if a person doesn't tell one of her parents, there's a reason why, and it's a lot deeper than the law knows. The law isn't in the home."

In Minnesota, only 50 percent of minors live with both their natural parents, and yet all minors must notify *both* biological parents, or like Pam go to court for a "judicial bypass." If a parent is deceased, the minor must obtain a death certificate, show an obituary or provide some other corroboration of the death. If a parent's whereabouts are unknown, she must send a certified letter to the last known address and then wait forty-eight hours before obtaining an abortion. The only exceptions allowed are for "emancipated" minors (a category that has no strict legal definition and is therefore seldom invoked) and minors who are victims of sexual or physical abuse. Yet although a young woman who says she has been abused by a parent doesn't have to notify her parents before getting an abortion, the abuse *does* have to be reported to the child protection agency or the welfare department, which are legally bound to conduct an investigation. The feared (and probably real) consequence is that the abusive parent will learn not only of the abortion, but of being reported for abuse.

So, although individual judges may be lenient, Minnesota law itself is very strict and places a considerable burden on minors seeking a confidential abortion. Not all minors are able to sort out the bureaucratic requirements of the law or negotiate their way through a complicated court system. Not all minors have access to a car, essential in rural areas often many hours from the few judges who hear these cases. And since minors generally wait until later in their pregnancies to obtain abortions than do older women, the delays caused by reckoning with the law can become significant. For some minors, parental notification or consent laws are not just an obstacle; the laws, in effect if not in stated intent, severely restrict their access to safe, legal abortions.

Teen Abortions Rose

From 1981, when the Minnesota law was first enacted, until 1986, when the statute was overturned in U.S. District Court, the birthrate among minors in Minneapolis, the city with the most complete data available, rose significantly. Minneapolis Health Department figures show that between 1981 and 1984, for example, the birthrate for fifteen- to seventeen-year-olds in Minneapolis increased 38.4 percent, while the birthrate among eighteen- and nineteen-year-olds, unaffected by the law, rose only 0.3 percent. During the same period, the number of abortions obtained by fifteen- to seventeen-year-olds in the state dropped 35 percent, though it's unclear whether this drop stems from the law (and the obstacles it places in the way of a teen who wants an abortion) or from independently declining abortion rates throughout the region.

Perhaps the most significant statistic, however, is that among those Minnesota minors who did obtain abortions while the law was in effect, there was a 26.5 percent increase in later, more costly, higher-risk second-trimester abortions. This increase runs contrary to national trends.

Sponsors of parental notification and consent laws maintain that they are not intended to restrict a minor's right to an abortion, which is guaranteed by *Roe v. Wade*. Rather, they argue, the purpose of the law is to improve family communication. Gene Waldorf, the Minnesota state senator who was the chief sponsor of the law, believes abortion should be illegal, but, he insists "The primary purpose of this law is to get whatever parental support is possible for the teenager. I don't know any parents that aren't most likely to stand by their kids when they are in trouble. We shouldn't write laws around the rarest, poorest kind of parental performance."

Encouraging Parental Support

Jackie Schwietz, codirector of Minnesota Citizens Concerned for Life, the group that drafted Minnesota's law and found sponsors for it, says, "The law is intended to encourage the support and counsel of parents at a time of crucial decision making for a daughter. No matter how mature a minor is, her responses and thought processes are not what an adult's are. She needs help, ideally from a parent, not from some third party who has no real interest in her. Whether a girl has an abortion or not, the parents need to know what they are dealing with in case there are emotional or physical consequences. The law gives parents a chance to investigate clinics and doctors, to give better medical histories. It's a law that encourages more thought about a difficult decision."

Judging from several recent national surveys, this argument has proved persuasive. Although all the parental notice/consent laws passed to date have been drafted by anti-choice groups, they enjoy widespread support among otherwise pro-choice adults. In poll after poll, over 70 percent of Americans consistently say they do not want to see *Roe v. Wade* overturned, yet the same high percentage approve of parental notification laws for minors.

"I think parents have a very difficult time accepting that a child may not turn to them in a time of need," says Tina Welsh, director of the Women's Health Center in Duluth. "We would like to believe that moms and dads are caring. Even abusive parents have a lot invested in the myth of the traditional, loving, caring family. But anyone who works professionally with children knows the intact, caring family is the exception rather than the rule. I raised foster children for ten years. I know not all parents are caring parents. Besides, it's not just abuse that makes the girls not want to involve their parents. Often they feel they don't want to place additional stress on an unemployed father or a sick mother. They may intend to tell their parents later, but not at the time of sorrow or stress."

Law for "Perfect Families"

Heather Pearson, who at age fourteen went to court in Minneapolis to avoid notifying her father, whom she rarely saw, agree. "These laws are made for those perfect families. Well, where are those perfect families?" Now twenty, Heather is still furious about her experience in court. "It was humiliating, degrading. I had my mom's approval, and she was the one I considered my parent. So why did I have to tell such personal things to a judge? There are families that just can't communicate, and for reasons *that are nobody's business.*"

Minnesota Judge Allen Oleisky, who heard 1,500 cases like Heather's in the 1980s, agrees that these hearings are pointless and said so in U.S. District Court when the law was under review. In fact, none of the Minnesota judges, public defenders or health professionals involved in implementing the law between 1981 and 1986 could testify to any positive effect from it. Judge [Gerald] Martin, when asked his opinion of the law shortly after hearing [a] case, was unequivocal: "I don't see any benefit to anybody. Every judge I know of who has heard these cases, no matter what his political or religious persuasion, has found that the law is not serving any positive purpose. Its only practical purpose might be to deter a young woman from exercising her choice."

At the heart of the debate over parental notice and consent laws are diametrically opposed views of what the typical American family is like in the 1990s. Do Mom and Dad really know best? Can they be trusted to act in the best interest of their minor child? Or are they just as likely to be absent, drug-dependent, uninterested or abusive? Supporters of these laws see the 50 percent of Minnesota minors who come from intact families. Opponents see the 50 percent who come from broken homes or dysfunctional families. . . .

Caught in the Cross Fire

Caught in the cross fire are . . . the twelve minors who sought abortions at the Meadowbrook Women's Clinic in suburban

Minneapolis one week last fall [1990] shortly after Minnesota's parental notification law had been put back into effect. Not all of them wished to talk about their decision, but those who did told stories that demonstrate how various and unpredictable the impact of this law can be.

Laura, seventeen, a college-bound senior who wants to study medicine, came to the clinic seeking her second abortion. The first time she became pregnant, before the law had been upheld by the Supreme Court, she freely chose to talk with both her parents. "The way they reacted last time, I just don't want to do that again," said Laura. "Everyone says once you tell your parents, you'll find out how supportive they are. I thought my mom would be more of a friend, but she wasn't. She was hysterical; she only asked once in two weeks how I felt, physically or emotionally. When I told my dad, he said; 'So what are you going to name it?' He just joked about it." . . .

So when she became pregnant a second time, despite her boyfriend's regular use of condoms, Laura came to the clinic rather than to her parents for counseling. "I feel real guilty," Laura said. "The first time I didn't use birth control, but this time I did and it makes me feel even worse, I thought I can't have another abortion, because of the pain last time. Not physical pain, but like, when it was my projected due date and I'm thinking, 'Oh, it could have been born today.' And that makes me know I could never give a baby up for adoption. But my boyfriend is very standoffish this time, and I don't know how I could raise a child myself. I'm not sure it's the right decision, but I have to go with my impulse now."

Despite her fear that "the judge might treat me as if this is just a form of birth control for me," Laura chose to talk to him rather than her parents. "I talked to them last time, and it's made me turn away from them more." The judge granted her request for a bypass; she had an abortion the same day.

Legislating Communication

Because she did not discover her pregnancy until the eighteenth week, Beth, seventeen, and her divorced mother, Joan, immediately notified Beth's father that she was seeking an abortion. Joan, knowing the health risks of late abortions, felt they could not afford the delay involved in getting a judicial bypass. Both mother and daughter, for different reasons, resent the law that forced them to notify Beth's father, who is remarried and lives in another part of the country.

"I would have told my mom anyway," Beth said, "because she's the one who is there for me. And I would have told my dad, but not immediately, and not over the phone. . . ."

As Beth talked, it was clear that she deeply desires a closer relationship with her father and has struggled hard to build one, but the law, by forcing premature communication, backfired on her. "It was a real setback," Beth said. "All he said was, 'Okay, okay, I'll send the [acknowledgment] letter tomorrow.' He didn't ask how I was doing. It was tough, real tough, because I felt so out, so gone. It felt so much like he didn't care."

If Beth sounded hurt, her single, working mother sounded furious. "Beth's father doesn't have a damn thing to do with how we live. He provides financial support and THAT IS IT! He claims he loves our daughters, and I think in his way he does, but the emotional support is just not there. Not for them. Not for me. That's the other part of this. The law forced me to deal with someone who doesn't want to deal with me. That's not fair."

Making Things Worse

Julie, fifteen, tried to talk to her mother about her pregnancy. She didn't want to, but because of the law, she made an effort. The results were so disastrous that she ended up going to court for a judicial bypass anyway. . . .

Before making the decision to abort, Julie talked to her doctor, her high school counselor and her boyfriend's parents, who are paying for the abortion. "My mom said, 'This is a lesson you have to learn.' But you can't learn a lesson when you're dealing with someone else's life. I'm not going to mess up my baby's life because my mom thinks I have to learn a lesson. That's not right at all. If I was going to carry it to term, I would never give it up to anybody, because I'd be wondering about it for the rest of my life. But I can't keep a baby either. I wouldn't be able to afford it. I wouldn't be able to go to school. I probably wouldn't even be a good mother because I'm not totally grown-up yet myself. I'm not going to try to be a mother to my baby and to myself too. That's too much. I can't do both. I've thought a lot about it. I had to" . . .

Law Does Not Do What It Intends

In none of the cases at the Meadowbrook Clinic that week had the law served its stated purpose—to improve communications and strengthen families. Those parents and children who could talk openly to one another did so independently of the law; where poor communication existed, the law either made a bad situation worse or placed the additional burden of a court hearing on an already troubled minor.

Paula Wendt, director of the Meadowbrook Clinic, says an inordinate amount of her staff's time—time that might be spent on much-needed counseling—is consumed explaining the law to minors and helping them arrange hearings. In her mind, the law is a form of harassment—the legal equivalent of the picketers who sometimes fill the hallway outside the clinic.

Like many others. Wendt thinks notification laws are the wedge anti-choice groups are using to break the pro-choice consensus in this country. "They're masterful," she says. "They know how to chip away at the women who are least able to defend themselves, poor women on Medicaid and minors without a vote, women who can't fight for themselves yet."

"I always took legislators much more seriously," she adds. "But they write these laws and they pass these laws and they don't care about their effects. They don't make any arrangements to see that bypass hearings are really available. They don't care if they're workable and fair. I'm over forty, and I'm disillusioned. What must these young women feel?"

An Illogical Law

The illogic of the law is what most bothers Duluth clinic director Tina Welsh. "The reasoning behind this bill drives me crazy," she says. "It presumes a minor is not mature enough to make a decision to end a pregnancy, but in nine months she will be mature enough to have a child and make all the decisions for its welfare."

Suzanne, a single, working mother of four and grandmother to the infant her oldest daughter bore at age fifteen, feels she is a victim of that illogic. "I'm appalled that we have a law that requires notification of a minor's parents for an abortion but not for a pregnancy that will be carried to term," she says. "Since I am now supporting my grandchild, and am *required* to under the laws of Minnesota [as long as her daughter is a minor and lives at home], I feel that I should have been involved in my daughter's decision. But she was counseled at a pro-life clinic not to let me know she was pregnant, because I might try to influence her to have an abortion. I resent this. I've been struggling as a single parent, with practically no child support, for ten years, and now I'm a single grandparent, with practically no child support.

"It's been just devastating to us," says Suzanne, who discovered her daughter's pregnancy by accident in the twenty-sixth week. "I spent last night holding this sobbing sixteen-year-old girl who doesn't know if she can make it. She is an excellent little parent, but she didn't understand what caring for a baby meant, what it would cost us, how her life would utterly change. She has talked about suicide. She says, 'My life is nothing now,' and I live with a very real fear for her. I think it's a hideous insult to have a law that forces minors to reveal their abortions but allows them to hide their pregnancies. Who is protected by that law? Not me or my daughter. Our family is in real danger."

> "Roughly 3,600 girls [seeking abortions]
> . . . went to court rather than notify
> their parents, and fewer than 10 had
> their petitions denied."

Parental Notification Laws Do Little to Curb Teen Abortion

David Whitman

David Whitman, a writer and author, covered social policy for U.S. News & World Report from 1985 to 2003. He has written extensively on abortion, poverty, welfare reform, ethnicity and race, family policy, and other social trends.

In the following viewpoint, Whitman argues that a Minnesota state law requiring parental involvement for minors considering abortion has had little effect on the rate of teenage abortions in the 1980s.

Among liberals and conservatives, nothing rousts the Chicken Littles quite as fast as a Supreme Court hearing on abortion. This week [early December 1989], the Court considers a challenge to a Minnesota statute that requires minors to notify both parents before obtaining an abortion, and, as usual, the Justices will hear portentous warnings about what will happen if they uphold it—or strike it down. Lawyers from the American Civil Liberties Union [ACLU] claim that the law had a "catastrophic impact" upon minors' right to abortion. Pro-life backers, meanwhile, defend the law for fostering vital parental involvement and saving lives.

David Whitman, "When Pregnant Girls Face Mom and Dad," *U.S. News & World Report*, vol. 107, December 4, 1989, p. 25–26. Copyright © 1989 U.S. News and World Report, L.P. All rights reserved. Reprinted with permission.

The contradictory claims in the Minnesota case are noteworthy, since they involve one of the most contentious issues related to abortion—the role parents should play when their daughters get pregnant—and because the Court, at last, has a genuine opportunity to evaluate the assertions of both camps. In considering *Hodgson v. Minnesota*, named for Jane Hodgson, the obstetrician who challenged the state law, the Court will have real-life data on which to base its judgment. And the data show that Minnesota's tough law neither accomplished the goals of its pro-life supporters nor fulfilled the fears of pro-choice opponents. Instead, it appears to have had a modest impact. That suggests future laws spawned by the *Webster* [*v. Reproductive Services* (1989)] decision, which allowed the states greater leeway in restricting abortions, may do surprisingly little to curb abortions.

The fact that there are statistics in the Minnesota case makes it different from virtually all of its predecessors. Ever since the Court granted women the right to abortion in *Roe v. Wade* in 1973, abortion-related statutes reviewed by the Court have typically been enforced only briefly, if at all, or have had little practical significance because women side-stepped them by going to states with more permissive policies. By contrast, Minnesota's parental-notification law was enforced from 1981 until 1986, when a U.S. district judge struck it down. It affected more than 16,000 pregnant teens, and the state meticulously tracked teenage abortions and births while the law was in effect.

Most Americans Support Notification

When the law was drafted, proponents argued parents should know if their teenage daughter was going to have an abortion, just as surely as they should know that a doctor was planning to remove her tonsils. Indeed, polls show about 70 percent of Americans support that position. But the Minnesota statute was unusually stringent. Unlike other such laws, it required minors to notify *both* biological parents, with no exceptions provided for divorce, separation or even abandonment. It did provide an alternative: Instead of telling their parents, pregnant girls could petition a judge to approve an abortion, a "judicial bypass" procedure endorsed in several Supreme Court rulings.

Pro-choice activists warned that the law would lead to suicides and dangerous self-abortions. Pregnant girls, they predicted, would be tossed out of their homes by angry parents or, more likely, forced to bear unwanted babies. Yet the state's data do not back up those dire predictions. Between 1981 and 1986, when the law was in effect, the number of out-of-wedlock births to Minnesota minors did not rise, while pregnancy, abortion and birth rates for minors all modestly declined. State officials say that notification did not lead to a single known incident where parents violently abused their daughter; forced her to have an abortion; prevented her from having one, or created medical problems for her by delaying one.

At the same time, the predictions of pro-lifers also failed to materialize. The notification requirements did not significantly reduce the propensity of pregnant teenagers to seek abortions. In 1980, roughly 54 percent of pregnant Minnesota minors had abortions; in 1986, the last year of the law, just over 49 percent did. Even the prospect of going before a judge did not seem to deter girls. Roughly 3,600 girls—about half of those who had abortions while the law was in effect—went to court rather than notify their parents, and fewer than 10 had their petitions denied. Thomas Webber, executive director of Minnesota Planned Parenthood, says that the law "plainly did not return minors to a state of blissful chastity."

Legislating Parental Support

The pro-lifers' other goal in enacting the Minnesota law was to "bring back some loving parental support," according to

Gene Waldorf, the state senator who authored the bill. And while the data are not definitive, it does appear that the law increased the percentage of families where *both* parents found out about a minor daughter's pending abortion—about half the cases. Yet the law appears to have worsened parent-child communication, especially for teens from single-parent homes, by generating new *Angst*, fears and tears. Often, such teenagers chose to notify a judge with their mothers by their side, instead of reinvolving a father who may have had little or no contact with them for years. Some nervous teens vomited during the court proceedings, one began to self-abort spontaneously. And one girl, whose father was a prominent pro-life politician, contemplated suicide before petitioning a judge for an abortion.

Still, it is hard to pin down the effects of any abortion statute, even one that was carefully monitored. There is no way to know whether the Minnesota law might have improved communication between some minors and parents, because daughters who talked to their parents and then decided to keep their babies would not end up teary eyed in court or at a clinic. Similarly, the drop in pregnancy, abortion and birth rates among minors in Minnesota from 1981 to 1986 might be due to increased use of contraceptives or greater awareness of sexually transmitted diseases, rather than parental notice. (In fact, a parallel decline took place in Minnesota over the same time in the birth-and-abortion rates of 18 and 19-year-olds not covered by the law.)

If the Supreme Court directly overturns *Roe*, Minnesota and other states could someday implement an anti-abortion statute that does severely restrict the right to abortion. Some pro-choice activists fear *Hodgson* may eventually lead to that, particularly since an out-of-court settlement was reached last week [November 1989] in a key abortion-restriction case in Illinois that the Court had planned to hear. Rachael Pine, an attorney for the ACLU, says that the very popularity of parental-involvement laws could make it "easier for the Court to chip away at *Roe* in the context of the abortion rights of minors."

But most legal experts doubt the Court will reconsider *Roe* in *Hodgson*. The Justices have already upheld several parental-consent laws without challenging *Roe*. And 31 states have passed consent or notification laws (although 19 of those are either unenforced, enjoined by courts or declared unconstitutional, mostly because they lack an expeditious and confidential bypass procedure). The most likely outcome of a Court ruling upholding Minnesota's law is that parental-involvement statutes would proliferate and be enforced in much of the nation. Judging from Minnesota's experience, the laws might have surprisingly little impact on the right to abortion, no matter what the apostles of doom predict.

CHAPTER 3

Implementing the "Undue Burden" Standard

Case Overview

Planned Parenthood of Southeastern Pennsylvania v. Casey (1992)

Planned Parenthood of Southeastern Pennsylvania v. Casey (1992) challenged the constitutionality of five provisions of the Pennsylvania Abortion Control Act of 1982. The plaintiffs consisted of four abortion clinics, a doctor representing himself, and a class of physicians who provided abortion services. The first provision, informed consent, required physicians to inform women about possible health risks and complications from having an abortion at least twenty-four hours before the abortion was performed. The second provision, spousal notification, required married women to sign a statement indicating that she had informed her husband of the abortion. A third provision required minors to obtain written parental consent before receiving an abortion, but it offered a judicial bypass for minors who could not notify their parents. A fourth provision imposed a twenty-four-hour waiting period before a woman could receive an abortion, and a fifth provision required that abortion providers follow onerous reporting protocols. The district court had found all the provisions to be unconstitutional.

In the Supreme Court's plurality opinion, written by Sandra Day O'Connor, the Supreme Court upheld what it called "the essential holding" of *Roe v. Wade*, that the right to abortion is grounded in the Due Process Clause of the Fourteenth Amendment. The Court emphasized the need for *stare decisis*, or the precedent of the Court's prior decisions, even if those decisions were unpopular, and the importance of maintaining consistency despite changes in the personnel of the Supreme Court.

Even though the Court emphasized the need to respect *stare decisis*, it nevertheless overturned a few aspects of *Roe v. Wade*. Perhaps most importantly, the Court overturned the strict trimester formula used in *Roe* to balance a woman's interest in obtaining an abortion against the State's interest in the life of the fetus. By 1992 medical advances were such that a fetus could be considered viable, or able to survive outside the womb, much earlier in the pregnancy than in 1972, when *Roe* was decided. Additionally, the Court discarded the concept of "strict scrutiny," which meant that the woman's fundamental right to abortion could only be restricted by compelling government interest.

Instead, the Court declared that laws restricting abortion were constitutional unless they created an "undue burden" for the woman seeking an abortion and the providers of an abortion. The Court defined an "undue burden" as having "the purpose in effect of placing a substantial obstacle in the path of a woman seeking an abortion of a nonviable fetus." Using the "undue burden" standard, the Court upheld the Pennsylvania abortion law's twenty-four-hour waiting period, informed consent counseling legislation, parental consent requirements, and mandated provider-reporting procedures, maintaining that none of these constituted an undue burden. The Court found, however, that the spousal notification requirement did constitute an undue burden, stating that it gave too much power to husbands over their wives and would exacerbate domestic violence.

The *Casey* decision is important in the history of the abortion debate for several reasons: 1) the *Roe* trimester reasoning—in which the state could not restrict abortion during the first trimester—was abandoned for the reasoning of "undue burden," in which the state could not place an unreasonable restriction on a woman's constitutional right to an abortion; 2) it was a divided Court, in that except for the opening three sections of the plurality opinion written by Justices O'Connor,

Anthony Kennedy, and David Souter, no other sections of any opinion were joined by a majority of justices. Third, at the time of *Planned Parenthood v. Casey*, only two of the justices sitting on the Supreme Court were known supporters of *Roe*— Harry Blackmun, who wrote the *Roe* majority decision, and John Paul Stevens, who had specifically affirmed *Roe* in past cases. The Court consisted of eight Republican-appointed justices, five of whom had been appointed by presidents Ronald Reagan or George H.W. Bush, who were strongly opposed to *Roe*. The only remaining Democratic appointee, Byron White, had penned a scathing dissent to the original *Roe* decision.

> "The woman's liberty is not so unlim-
> ited ... the State cannot show its con-
> cern for the life of the unborn."

Plurality Opinion: State Laws That Restrict Abortion Are Not Unconstitutional

Sandra Day O'Connor

*Sandra Day O'Connor was the first woman appointed to the Su-
preme Court. After graduating with honors from Stanford Law
School, where she served on the law review, she found that no
law firm wanted to hire her except as a legal secretary, so she accepted a job in public service and then started her own law firm
and became active in the Republican Party. Before becoming a
judge in 1974, O'Connor served briefly in the U.S. Senate. President Ronald Reagan appointed her to the Supreme Court in
1981 to replace Potter Stewart, who had retired. O'Connor herself retired in 2006.*

Delivering the opinion of the Supreme Court in Planned
Parenthood of Southeastern Pennsylvania v. Casey *(1992) in a
5-4 ruling, O'Connor upholds* Roe v. Wade *(1973) and maintains that state laws banning abortion would be unconstitutional. The Court abandons, however, the trimester framework
of* Roe v. Wade *in favor of the "undue burden standard." Undue
burden is defined as a "substantial obstacle in the path of a
woman seeking the abortion of a nonviable fetus." Applying this
rule to the provisions at issue, the Court finds that mandatory
counseling about the health risks of abortion and the probable*

Sandra Day O'Connor, plurality opinion, *Planned Parenthood of Southeastern Pennsylvania v. Casey*, U.S. Supreme Court, June 29, 1992.

gestational age of the fetus, a twenty-four-hour waiting period, parental notification requirements, and physician reporting do not constitute an "undue burden" on a woman seeking an abortion. The Court finds that only the spousal consent provision presents an undue burden. This case is significant because it is the current standard employed by the Court in deciding laws restricting abortion. The ruling has enabled states to pass more laws restricting access to abortion.

Men and women of good conscience can disagree, and we suppose some always shall disagree, about the profound moral and spiritual implications of terminating a pregnancy, even in its earliest stage. Some of us as individuals find abortion offensive to our most basic principles of morality, but that cannot control our decision. Our obligation is to define the liberty of all, not to mandate our own moral code. The underlying constitutional issue is whether the State can resolve these philosophic questions in such a definitive way that a woman lacks all choice in the matter, except perhaps in those rare circumstances in which the pregnancy is itself a danger to her own life or health, or is the result of rape or incest. . . .

Our law affords constitutional protection to personal decisions relating to marriage, procreation, contraception, family relationships, child rearing, and education. Our cases recognize the right of the individual, married or single, to be free from unwarranted governmental intrusion into matters so fundamentally affecting a person as the decision whether to bear or beget a child. Our precedents "have respected the private realm of family life which the state cannot enter." These matters, involving the most intimate and personal choices a person may make in a lifetime, choices central to personal dignity and autonomy, are central to the liberty protected by the Fourteenth Amendment. At the heart of liberty is the right to define one's own concept of existence, of meaning, of the universe, and of the mystery of human life. Beliefs about these matters could not define the attributes of personhood were they formed under compulsion of the State. . . .

Line Drawn at Viability

[I]t follows that it is a constitutional liberty of the woman to have some freedom to terminate her pregnancy. We conclude that the basic decision in *Roe* was based on a constitutional analysis which we cannot now repudiate. The woman's liberty is not so unlimited, however, that, from the outset, the State cannot show its concern for the life of the unborn and, at a later point in fetal development, the State's interest in life has sufficient force so that the right of the woman to terminate the pregnancy can be restricted.

That brings us, of course, to the point where much criticism has been directed at *Roe*, a criticism that always inheres when the Court draws a specific rule from what in the Constitution is but a general standard. We conclude, however, that the urgent claims of the woman to retain the ultimate control over her destiny and her body, claims implicit in the meaning of liberty, require us to perform that function. Liberty must not be extinguished for want of a line that is clear. And it falls to us to give some real substance to the woman's liberty to determine whether to carry her pregnancy to full term.

We conclude the line should be drawn at viability, so that, before that time, the woman has a right to choose to terminate her pregnancy. We adhere to this principle for two reasons. First, as we have said, is the doctrine of *stare decisis*. Any judicial act of line-drawing may seem somewhat arbitrary, but *Roe* was a reasoned statement, elaborated with great care. We have twice reaffirmed it in the face of great opposition. . . .

Protecting Potential Life

The second reason is that the concept of viability, as we noted in *Roe* is the time at which there is a realistic possibility of maintaining and nourishing a life outside the womb, so that the independent existence of the second life can, in reason and all fairness, be the object of state protection that now overrides the rights of the woman. Consistent with other constitutional norms, legislatures may draw lines which appear arbitrary without the necessity of offering a justification. But courts may not. We must justify the lines we draw. And there is no line other than viability which is more workable. To be sure, as we have said, there may be some medical developments that affect the precise point of viability, but this is an imprecision within tolerable limits, given that the medical community and all those who must apply its discoveries will continue to explore the matter. The viability line also has, as a practical matter, an element of fairness. In some broad sense, it might be said that a woman who fails to act before viability has consented to the State's intervention on behalf of the developing child.

The woman's right to terminate her pregnancy before viability is the most central principle of *Roe v. Wade*. It is a rule of law and a component of liberty we cannot renounce.

On the other side of the equation is the interest of the State in the protection of potential life. The *Roe* Court recognized the State's "important and legitimate interest in protecting the potentiality of human life." The weight to be given this state interest, not the strength of the woman's interest, was the difficult question faced in *Roe*. We do not need to say whether each of us, had we been Members of the Court when the valuation of the state interest came before it as an original matter, would have concluded, as the *Roe* Court did, that its weight is insufficient to justify a ban on abortions prior to viability even when it is subject to certain exceptions. The matter is not before us in the first instance, and, coming as it does after nearly 20 years of litigation in *Roe*'s wake we are satisfied that the immediate question is not the soundness of *Roe*'s resolution of the issue, but the precedential force that must be accorded to its holding. And we have concluded that the essential holding of *Roe* should be reaffirmed.

Difficulties of Trimester Framework

Yet it must be remembered that *Roe v. Wade* speaks with clarity in establishing not only the woman's liberty but also the State's "important and legitimate interest in potential life." That portion of the decision in *Roe* has been given too little acknowledgment and implementation by the Court in its subsequent cases. Those cases decided that any regulation touching upon the abortion decision must survive strict scrutiny, to be sustained only if drawn in narrow terms to further a compelling state interest. Not all of the cases decided under that formulation can be reconciled with the holding in *Roe* itself that the State has legitimate interests in the health of the woman and in protecting the potential life within her. In resolving this tension, we choose to rely upon *Roe*, as against the later cases.

Roe established a trimester framework to govern abortion regulations. Under this elaborate but rigid construct, almost no regulation at all is permitted during the first trimester of pregnancy; regulations designed to protect the woman's health, but not to further the State's interest in potential life, are permitted during the second trimester; and, during the third trimester, when the fetus is viable, prohibitions are permitted provided the life or health of the mother is not at stake. Most of our cases since *Roe* have involved the application of rules derived from the trimester framework.

The trimester framework no doubt was erected to ensure that the woman's right to choose not become so subordinate to the State's interest in promoting fetal life that her choice exists in theory, but not in fact. We do not agree, however, that the trimester approach is necessary to accomplish this objective. A framework of this rigidity was unnecessary, and, in its later interpretation, sometimes contradicted the State's permissible exercise of its powers.

Though the woman has a right to choose to terminate or continue her pregnancy before viability, it does not at all follow that the State is prohibited from taking steps to ensure that this choice is thoughtful and informed. Even in the earliest stages of pregnancy, the State may enact rules and regulations designed to encourage her to know that there are philosophic and social arguments of great weight that can be brought to bear in favor of continuing the pregnancy to full term, and that there are procedures and institutions to allow adoption of unwanted children as well as a certain degree of state assistance if the mother chooses to raise the child herself. . . . It follows that States are free to enact laws to provide a reasonable framework for a woman to make a decision that has such profound and lasting meaning. This, too, we find consistent with *Roe*'s central premises, and indeed the inevitable consequence of our holding that the State has an interest in protecting the life of the unborn.

Rejecting the Trimester Framework

We reject the trimester framework, which we do not consider to be part of the essential holding of *Roe*. Measures aimed at ensuring that a woman's choice contemplates the consequences for the fetus do not necessarily interfere with the right recognized in *Roe*, although those measures have been found to be inconsistent with the rigid trimester framework announced in that case. A logical reading of the central holding in *Roe* itself, and a necessary reconciliation of the liberty of the woman and the interest of the State in promoting prenatal life, require, in our view, that we abandon the trimester framework as a rigid prohibition on all pre-viability regulation aimed at the protection of fetal life. The trimester framework suffers from these basic flaws: in its formulation, it misconceives the nature of the pregnant woman's interest; and in practice, it undervalues the State's interest in potential life, as recognized in *Roe*.

As our jurisprudence relating to all liberties save perhaps abortion has recognized, not every law which makes a right more difficult to exercise is, ipso facto, an infringement of that right. An example clarifies the point. We have held that not every ballot access limitation amounts to an infringement of the right to vote. Rather, the States are granted substantial flexibility in establishing the framework within which voters choose the candidates for whom they wish to vote.

The abortion right is similar. Numerous forms of state regulation might have the incidental effect of increasing the cost or decreasing the availability of medical care, whether for abortion or any other medical procedure. The fact that a law which serves a valid purpose, one not designed to strike at the right itself, has the incidental effect of making it more difficult or more expensive to procure an abortion cannot be enough to invalidate it. Only where state regulation imposes an undue burden on a woman's ability to make this decision does the power of the State reach into the heart of the liberty protected by the Due Process Clause.

The Undue Burden Standard

For the most part, the Court's early abortion cases adhered to this view. In *Maher v. Roe* (1977), the Court explained: *Roe* did not declare an unqualified "constitutional right to an abortion," as the District Court seemed to think. Rather, the right protects the woman from unduly burdensome interference with her freedom to decide whether to terminate her pregnancy.

These considerations of the nature of the abortion right illustrate that it is an overstatement to describe it as a right to decide whether to have an abortion "without interference from the State." All abortion regulations interfere to some degree with a woman's ability to decide whether to terminate her pregnancy. It is, as a consequence, not surprising that, despite the protestations contained in the original *Roe* opinion to the effect that the Court was not recognizing an absolute right, the Court's experience applying the trimester framework has led to the striking down of some abortion regulations which in no real sense deprived women of the ultimate decision. Those decisions went too far, because the right recognized by *Roe* is a right to be free from unwarranted governmental intrusion into matters so fundamentally affecting a person as the decision whether to bear or beget a child. Not all governmental intrusion is, of necessity, unwarranted, and that brings us to the other basic flaw in the trimester framework: even in *Roe*'s terms, in practice, it undervalues the State's interest in the potential life within the woman.

Roe v. Wade was express in its recognition of the State's important and legitimate interest[s] in preserving and protecting the health of the pregnant woman [and] in protecting the potentiality of human life. The trimester framework, however, does not fulfill Roe's own promise that the State has an interest in protecting fetal life or potential life. *Roe* began the contradiction by using the trimester framework to forbid any regulation of abortion designed to advance that interest before viability. Before viability, *Roe* and subsequent cases treat all governmental attempts to influence a woman's decision on behalf of the potential life within her as unwarranted. This treatment is, in our judgment, incompatible with the recognition that there is a substantial state interest in potential life throughout pregnancy.

The very notion that the State has a substantial interest in potential life leads to the conclusion that not all regulations must be deemed unwarranted. Not all burdens on the right to decide whether to terminate a pregnancy will be undue. In our view, the undue burden standard is the appropriate means of reconciling the State's interest with the woman's constitutionally protected liberty. . . .

A finding of an undue burden is a shorthand for the conclusion that a state regulation has the purpose or effect of placing a substantial obstacle in the path of a woman seeking an abortion of a nonviable fetus. A statute with this purpose is invalid because the means chosen by the State to further the interest in potential life must be calculated to inform the woman's free choice, not hinder it. And a statute which, while furthering the interest in potential life or some other valid state interest, has the effect of placing a substantial obstacle in the path of a woman's choice cannot be considered a permissible means of serving its legitimate ends. . . . If considered judgment, an undue burden is an unconstitutional burden. Understood another way, we answer the question, left open in previous opinions discussing the undue burden formulation, whether a law designed to further the State's interest in fetal life which imposes an undue burden on the woman's decision before fetal viability could be constitutional. The answer is no.

Guiding Principles

Some guiding principles should emerge. What is at stake is the woman's right to make the ultimate decision, not a right to be insulated from all others in doing so. Regulations which do no more than create a structural mechanism by which the State, or the parent or guardian of a minor, may express profound respect for the life of the unborn are permitted, if they are not a substantial obstacle to the woman's exercise of the right to choose. Unless it has that effect on her right of choice, a state measure designed to persuade her to choose childbirth over abortion will be upheld if reasonably related to that goal. Regulations designed to foster the health of a woman seeking an abortion are valid if they do not constitute an undue burden.

Even when jurists reason from shared premises, some disagreement is inevitable. That is to be expected in the application of any legal standard which must accommodate life's complexity. We do not expect it to be otherwise with respect to the undue burden standard. We give this summary:

(a) To protect the central right recognized by *Roe v. Wade* while at the same time accommodating the State's profound interest in potential life, we will employ the undue burden analysis as explained in this opinion. An undue burden exists, and therefore a provision of law is invalid, if its purpose or effect is to place a substantial obstacle in the path of a woman seeking an abortion before the fetus attains viability.

(b) We reject the rigid trimester framework of *Roe v. Wade*. To promote the State's profound interest in potential life, throughout pregnancy, the State may take measures to ensure that the woman's choice is informed, and measures designed to advance this interest will not be invalidated as long as their purpose is to persuade the woman to choose childbirth over abortion. These measures must not be an undue burden on the right.

(c) As with any medical procedure, the State may enact regulations to further the health or safety of a woman seeking an abortion. Unnecessary health regulations that have the purpose or effect of presenting a substantial obstacle to a woman seeking an abortion impose an undue burden on the right.

(d) Our adoption of the undue burden analysis does not disturb the central holding of *Roe v. Wade*, and we reaffirm that holding. Regardless of whether exceptions are made for particular circumstances, a State may not prohibit any woman from making the ultimate decision to terminate her pregnancy before viability.

(e) We also reaffirm *Roe*'s holding that, subsequent to viability, the State, in promoting its interest in the potentially of human life, may, if it chooses, regulate, and even proscribe, abortion except where it is necessary, in appropriate medical judgment, for the preservation of the life or health of the mother.

> "We believe that Roe was wrongly decided, and that it can and should be overruled."

Dissenting Opinion: *Roe v. Wade* Should Be Overturned

William Rehnquist

William Rehnquist served on the Supreme Court from 1972 until his death in 2005, having served for almost nineteen years of his tenure as chief justice. Prior to his appointment to the Supreme Court by President Richard Nixon, Rehnquist was active in the Republican Party in Arizona, serving as a legal advisor to Barry Goldwater's 1964 presidential campaign. Rehnquist was a strong proponent of federalism, or states' rights. In his opinion, the Court should not attempt to influence public policy by expanding the scope of the law beyond the framers' original intent.

Although he concurs in part with the Court's decision in Planned Parenthood of Southeastern Pennsylvania v. Casey *(1992), which upheld a woman's right to choose an abortion, in the following dissent Rehnquist argues that* Roe v. Wade *was wrongly decided and that the Court's definition of "liberty" in the Due Process Clause of the Fourteenth Amendment is overly broad. Furthermore, Rehnquist maintains, the fact that the American people have become accustomed to* Roe v. Wade *should not prevent the Court from correcting past errors and overturning* Roe, *as it has done in other historic cases, such as* Plessy v. Ferguson *(1896), which allowed "separate but equal" treatment for minorities.*

William Rehnquist, plurality opinion, *Planned Parenthood of Southeastern Pennsylvania v. Casey*, U.S. Supreme Court, June 29, 1992.

The joint opinion, following its newly minted variation on *stare decisis* [precedent], retains the outer shell of *Roe v. Wade*, (1973), but beats a wholesale retreat from the substance of that case. We believe that *Roe* was wrongly decided, and that it can and should be overruled consistently with our traditional approach to *stare decisis* in constitutional cases. We would adopt the approach of the plurality in *Webster v. Reproductive Health Services*, (1989) and uphold the challenged provisions of the Pennsylvania statute in their entirety. . . .

In construing the phrase "liberty" incorporated in the Due Process Clause of the Fourteenth Amendment, we have recognized that its meaning extends beyond freedom from physical restraint. In *Pierce v. Society of Sisters*, (1925), we held that it included a parent's right to send a child to private school; in *Meyer v. Nebraska*, (1923), we held that it included a right to teach a foreign language in a parochial school. Building on these cases, we have held that the term "liberty" includes a right to marry, *Loving v. Virginia*, (1967); a right to procreate, *Skinner v. Oklahoma ex rel. Williamson*, (1942); and a right to use contraceptives, *Griswold v. Connecticut*, (1965); *Eisenstadt v. Baird*, (1972). But a reading of these opinions makes clear that they do not endorse any all-encompassing "right of privacy."

Roe Defined "Privacy" Too Broadly

In *Roe v. Wade*, the Court recognized a "guarantee of personal privacy" which "is broad enough to encompass a woman's decision whether or not to terminate her pregnancy." We are now of the view that, in terming this right fundamental, the Court in *Roe* read the earlier opinions upon which it based its decision much too broadly. Unlike marriage, procreation, and contraception, abortion "involves the purposeful termination of a potential life." The abortion decision must therefore be recognized as *sui generis*, different in kind from the others that the Court has protected under the rubric of personal or family privacy and autonomy. One cannot ignore the fact that a woman is not isolated in her pregnancy, and that the decision to abort necessarily involves the destruction of a fetus.

Nor do the historical traditions of the American people support the view that the right to terminate one's pregnancy is "fundamental." The common law which we inherited from England made abortion after "quickening" an offense. At the time of the adoption of the Fourteenth Amendment, statutory prohibitions or restrictions on abortion were commonplace; in 1868, at least 28 of the then-37 States and 8 Territories had statutes banning or limiting abortion. By the turn of the . . . century, virtually every State had a law prohibiting or restricting abortion on its books. By the middle of the [20th] century, a liberalization trend had set in. But 21 of the restrictive abortion laws in effect in 1868 were still in effect in 1973 when *Roe* was decided, and an overwhelming majority of the States prohibited abortion unless necessary to preserve the life or health of the mother. On this record, it can scarcely be said that any deeply rooted tradition of relatively unrestricted abortion in our history supported the classification of the right to abortion as "fundamental" under the Due Process Clause of the Fourteenth Amendment.

We think, therefore, both in view of this history and of our decided cases dealing with substantive liberty under the Due Process Clause, that the Court was mistaken in *Roe* when it classified a woman's decision to terminate her pregnancy as a "fundamental right" that could be abridged only in a manner which withstood "strict scrutiny." . . .

We believe that the sort of constitutionally imposed abortion code of the type illustrated by our decisions following *Roe* is inconsistent "with the notion of a Constitution cast in general terms, as ours is, and usually speaking in general principles, as ours does." The Court in *Roe* reached too far when it analogized the right to abort a fetus to the rights involved in

Pierce, Meyer, Loving, and *Griswold,* and thereby deemed the right to abortion fundamental.

Court's Opinion Inconsistent

The joint opinion of Justices [Sandra Day] O'Connor, [Anthony] Kennedy, and [David] Souter cannot bring itself to say that *Roe* was correct as an original matter, but the authors are of the view that the immediate question is not the soundness of *Roe's* resolution of the issue, but the precedential force that must be accorded to its holding. Instead of claiming that *Roe* was correct as a matter of original constitutional interpretation, the opinion therefore contains an elaborate discussion of *stare decisis.* This discussion of the principle of *stare decisis* appears to be almost entirely dicta [nonbinding rulings], because the joint opinion does not apply that principle in dealing with *Roe. Roe* decided that a woman had a fundamental right to an abortion. The joint opinion rejects that view. *Roe* decided that abortion regulations were to be subjected to "strict scrutiny," and could be justified only in the light of "compelling state interests." The joint opinion rejects that view. *Roe* analyzed abortion regulation under a rigid trimester framework, a framework which has guided this Court's decisionmaking for 19 years. The joint opinion rejects that framework.

Stare decisis is defined in *Black's Law Dictionary* as meaning "to abide by, or adhere to, decided cases." Whatever the "central holding" of *Roe* that is left after the joint opinion finishes dissecting it is surely not the result of that principle. While purporting to adhere to precedent, the joint opinion instead revises it. *Roe* continues to exist, but only in the way a storefront on a western movie set exists: a mere facade to give the illusion of reality. Decisions following *Roe,* such as *Akron v. Akron Center for Reproductive Health, Inc.,* (1983), and *Thornburgh v. American College of Obstetricians and Gynecologists,* (1986), are frankly overruled in part under the "undue burden" standard expounded in the joint opinion.

In our view, authentic principles of *stare decisis* do not require that any portion of the reasoning in *Roe* be kept intact.

The joint opinion discusses several *stare decisis* factors which, it asserts, point toward retaining a portion of *Roe*. Two of these factors are that the main "factual underpinning" of *Roe* has remained the same, and that its doctrinal foundation is no weaker now than it was in 1973. Of course, what might be called the basic facts which gave rise to *Roe* have remained the same—women become pregnant, there is a point somewhere, depending on medical technology, where a fetus becomes viable, and women give birth to children. But this is only to say that the same facts which gave rise to *Roe* will continue to give rise to similar cases. It is not a reason, in and of itself, why those cases must be decided in the same incorrect manner as was the first case to deal with the question. And surely there is no requirement, in considering whether to depart from *stare decisis* in a constitutional case, that a decision be more wrong now than it was at the time it was rendered. If that were true, the most outlandish constitutional decision could survive forever, based simply on the fact that it was no more outlandish later than it was when originally rendered.

Not Precedent for Precedent's Sake

The joint opinion also points to the reliance interests involved in this context in its effort to explain why precedent must be followed for precedent's sake. . . . But, as the joint opinion apparently agrees, any traditional notion of reliance is not applicable here. The Court today cuts back on the protection afforded by *Roe*, and no one claims that this action defeats any reliance interest in the disavowed trimester framework. Similarly, reliance interests would not be diminished were the Court to go further and acknowledge the full error of *Roe*, as "reproductive planning could take virtually immediate account of" this action.

The joint opinion thus turns to what can only be described as an unconventional—and unconvincing—notion of reliance, a view based on the surmise that the availability of abortion since *Roe* has led to "two decades of economic and social developments" that would be undercut if the error of *Roe* were recognized. The joint opinion's assertion of this fact is undeveloped, and totally conclusory. In fact, one cannot be sure to what economic and social developments the opinion is referring. Surely it is dubious to suggest that women have reached their "places in society" in reliance upon *Roe*, rather than as a result of their determination to obtain higher education and compete with men in the job market, and of society's increasing recognition of their ability to fill positions that were previously thought to be reserved only for men.

In the end, having failed to put forth any evidence to prove any true reliance, the joint opinion's argument is based solely on generalized assertions about the national psyche, on a belief that the people of this country have grown accustomed to the *Roe* decision over the last 19 years and have "ordered their thinking and living around" it. As an initial matter, one might inquire how the joint opinion can view the "central holding" of *Roe* as so deeply rooted in our constitutional culture when it so casually uproots and disposes of that same decision's trimester framework. Furthermore, at various points in the past, the same could have been said about this Court's erroneous decisions that the Constitution allowed "separate but equal" treatment of minorities, or that "liberty" under the Due Process Clause protected "freedom of contract." The "separate but equal" doctrine lasted 58 years after *Plessy*, and *Lochner*'s protection of contractual freedom lasted 32 years. However, the simple fact that a generation or more had grown used to these major decisions did not prevent the Court from correcting its errors in those cases, nor should it prevent us from correctly interpreting the Constitution here. . . .

We therefore would hold that each of the challenged provisions of the Pennsylvania statute is consistent with the Constitution. It bears emphasis that our conclusion in this regard does not carry with it any necessary approval of these regulations. Our task is, as always, to decide only whether the challenged provisions of a law comport with the United States Constitution. If, as we believe, these do, their wisdom as a matter of public policy is for the people of Pennsylvania to decide.

> *"The justices said in effect, 'We are su-*
> *preme. We are masters—quiet, you*
> *little yahoos who think you have rights*
> *as citizens to make policy on abortion.'"*

The *Casey* Decision Is the Result of an Activist Court

Neil Munro

Neil Munro writes about the politics of science and the high-tech economy for National Journal.

In the following viewpoint, Munro discusses Planned Parenthood of Southeastern Pennsylvania v. Casey *(1992), which upheld* Roe v. Wade *(1973) and asserted as unconstitutional state laws that create an "undue burden" on a woman seeking abortion, as a declaration of judicial power. He cites conservatives who contend that although the Supreme Court has become more conservative since* Planned Parenthood v. Casey, *they do not believe that the Supreme Court will be any less activist than it has been.*

Moments after President [George W.] Bush introduced Samuel A. Alito Jr. as his Supreme Court nominee, advocates on the left and the right highlighted Alito's 1991 dissent as an appellate judge in the case *Planned Parenthood v. Casey.*

The huge impact of the Supreme Court's own landmark ruling on *Casey*, in 1992, gave Alito's dissent in the case—in

Neil Munro, "Alito and the Politics of *Casey*," *National Journal*, vol. 37, November 5, 2005, p. 34–35. Reproduced by permission.

which he said that Pennsylvania had the right to require women to notify their husbands of a scheduled abortion—political significance.

The high court upheld parts of a Pennsylvania law regulating abortion, while affirming the core of its 1973 *Roe v. Wade* decision. In their ruling, Justices Sandra Day O'Connor, Anthony Kennedy, and David Souter—all Republican appointees—made a point of rejecting Alito's argument in his dissent that Supreme Court precedents give state legislatures a right to require spousal notification.

But *Casey* reached beyond the volatile issue of abortion, legal scholars say. The ruling advocated a new, more libertarian outlook that the Supreme Court and lower courts have cited in striking down laws governing sodomy, marital rules, and sexual abuse, both liberals and conservatives say.

Casey Not Limited to Abortion

Casey affected "decisions about autonomy and family and self-definition and privacy ... [and was] not limited to abortion," says Louise Melling, director of the ACLU's [American Civil Liberties Union] project on reproductive freedom. She lauded the "very eloquent and moving passages about women in society" in the Supreme Court's *Casey* decision.

"*Casey* is a declaration of judicial power," says Ed Lazarus, a lawyer and legal author, and a former Supreme Court clerk for liberal Justice Harry Blackmun. In *Casey*, the justices were trying to accomplish two things, says Lazarus, who is now a senior counsel in the Los Angeles office of Akin, Gump, Strauss, Hauer & Feld: persuade voters to accept the Court's controversial abortion decisions, and resist pressure on the Court from politicians and the public.

After the *Casey* ruling, a majority of justices refused to hear any abortion-related cases until 2000, when they had to consider numerous state laws restricting "partial-birth" abortions. The Court struck down those laws, despite widespread public support for limits on late-term abortions.

Changing Court May Overturn *Casey*

Now, the impending retirement of O'Connor, the arrival of Chief Justice John Roberts, and the possible arrival of Alito threaten to overturn much of this *Casey* policy, Lazarus said.

To conservatives, the *Casey* decision has always represented the continuation of "the judicial power-grab" seen in *Roe*, says Ed Whelan, president of the Ethics and Public Policy Center.

Conservatives like Jan LaRue, chief counsel of Concerned Women for America, also argue that the Court's agenda in *Casey* went beyond abortion to promote a broad definition of personal rights. LaRue pointed to this statement in *Casey*: "At the heart of liberty is the right to define one's own concept of existence, of meaning, of the universe, and of the mystery of human life." But, LaRue says, that language "virtually permits anything imaginable [and] is used as a tool against the right of the American people to rule themselves, to set their own rules, and to enforce them."

In *Lawrence v. Texas*, a 2003 decision that further curbed legislative restrictions on sexual conduct, the majority cited the "heart of liberty" passage. The Massachusetts Supreme Court in turn cited *Lawrence* in its 2003 decision declaring unconstitutional the definition of marriage as the union of one man and one woman.

The Court Is Now Activist

In its *Casey* decision, the U.S. Supreme Court also showed it wanted to resist public opposition to its rulings, scholars say. Although the Court abandoned major elements of the *Roe* decision, it also declared that over-ruling the core abortion right embodied in *Roe* in the face of public opposition "would seriously weaken the Court's capacity to exercise the judicial power." In their *Casey* decision, justices also sought to reassure allies: "To all those who will be so tested by following [a court decision], the Court implicitly undertakes to remain steadfast, lest in the end a price be paid for nothing."

By declaring that the public and legislatures should defer to the Court's opinions, Whelan says, the justices said in effect, "We are supreme, we are masters—quiet, you little yahoos who think you have rights as citizens to make policy on abortion."

Lazarus says he doubts that the GOP-controlled Congress or President Bush will try to shrink the Supreme Court's role, despite the wishes of conservatives. Politicians want judges to implement their partisan agendas, he maintains, and he added that the media do not do investigative reports on the Court. Moreover, "the American people have come to accept the Court as an extraordinarily powerful political institution," Lazarus says. The Court's justices share this expansive view, and neither Chief Justice Roberts nor Alito, should he be confirmed, will give up this power, he says. [Samuel Alito joined the Supreme Court in 2006.]

| "Casey *opened the floodgates for eutha-*
nasia and other life-and-death issues."

In Devaluing the Life of the Fetus, *Casey* Paves the Way for Euthanasia

Charles Colson

Charles Colson is the founder of Prison Fellowship Ministries, a nonprofit organization devoted to outreach to convicts, victims of crime, and justice officers, for which he was awarded the Temple-ton Prize in 1993 for advancing the cause of religion. Chief counsel for President Richard Nixon from 1969 to 1973, Colson was named as one of the Watergate Seven and became interested in prison ministry and rehabilitation after serving time for con-spiring to cover up the Watergate burglary.

In the viewpoint below, Colson suggests that in connecting the right to abortion to a very broad notion of personal liberty, the Casey *decision (1992), which essentially upheld* Roe v. Wade *(1973), opens the door for doctor-assisted suicides and other life-and-death issues. Furthermore, he maintains that the Court dangerously applies religious language—and sacred status—to the individual act of abortion, conflating private beliefs and public policy.*

Two years ago in this space I described a genial dinner party that ended on a sour note. A Christian friend shocked me by promoting abortion as a solution to ghetto poverty. At that time, I warned readers that just such sincere,

Charles Colson, "*Casey* Strikes Out," *Christianity Today,* vol. 38, October 3, 1994 p. 104. Reproduced by permission of the author.

well-meaning people would start us down a slippery slide into a culture of death. Little did I realize how quickly that slide would become a free fall. In a mere 24 months, an extraordinary, shift has occurred that pushes us beyond abortion, beyond even the broader life issues, and into questions of whether we can maintain public order in a free society.

The shift was precipitated dramatically and unexpectedly by the Supreme Court's 1992 ruling *Planned Parenthood v. Casey*. Initially, both sides felt it was a middle-of-the-road decision. Pro-lifers were glad that the Court allowed states to impose some reasonable limits on abortion; pro-choicers that the Court reaffirmed the basic holding of *Roe v. Wade*.

But as the smoke cleared, it became obvious that the battle lines had shifted decisively. First, in *Roe* the Court had based abortion on the right to privacy, a right found nowhere explicitly in the Constitution—making the decision vulnerable to reversal. But in *Casey*, the Court transferred abortion from an implied to an explicit right—the right of liberty found in the Fourteenth Amendment—making the decision almost impossible to reverse.

Second, *Casey* opened the floodgates for euthanasia and other life-and-death issues. In pinning abortion to liberty, the Court defined *liberty* in the most sweeping terms conceivable—including, the majority said, "the most intimate and personal choices a person may make in a lifetime, choices central to personal dignity and autonomy."

Last May, U.S. District Judge Barbara Rothstein echoed that language when she struck down a Washington law prohibiting doctor-assisted suicide. Rothstein argued that suicide, like abortion, "involved the most intimate and personal choices a person may make," that it "constitutes a choice central to personal dignity and autonomy," and that it deserves the same "protection from unwarranted governmental interference."

Third, *Casey* set up personal autonomy as the rule in every area of life. In defining *liberty*, the majority waxed downright philosophical: "At the heart of liberty is the right to define one's own concept of existence, of meaning, of the universe, and of the mystery of human life."

At first sight, this passage may seem unremarkable. Beliefs about existence, meaning, and the mystery of human life are religious, and religious freedom is guaranteed by the First Amendment. What makes the passage revolutionary is that it applies religious language specifically to *abortion*. It gives religious status to a completely individualistic act: an act that presumes the right of one person to take the life of another for purely private reasons, without any public accountability. The Court endorsed a philosophy of the autonomous individual defining his or her own reality in complete isolation—even to the point of taking the life of another person.

But if autonomous, personal choices may not be circumscribed in any way by the state, the rule of law is impossible. In his dissenting opinion, Justice Scalia was prophetic: Under the Court's expansive definition, he warned, *liberty* could encompass "homosexual sodomy, polygamy, adult incest, and suicide."

But that list is altogether too short: The truth is that *liberty* could now encompass virtually any decision by which an individual expresses his sense of "selfhood," "meaning," and "existence."

As Christians, our response ought to be that all this talk about personal choices and meaning is irrelevant. Our courts and legal system are not concerned with private religious and metaphysical beliefs but with public justice. People of different beliefs—from Christmas to atheists to New Agers—may disagree vehemently over the meaning of life; yet we can all agree on standards of public justice and order, just as we can all agree to stop when the traffic signal is red.

We may hold different religious and philosophical *reasons* for stopping at the signal—different convictions regarding the source of moral authority. Christians hold a distinctive ethic that is based on Scripture and uniquely empowered by the indwelling Holy Spirit. Yet, as citizens we also contend for a public philosophy, justified by prudential arguments, aimed at promoting the public good.

The distinction between private belief and public philosophy is crucial if we are to maintain freedom of conscience and at the same time maintain public order. But it is precisely this distinction that *Casey* denied. It gave up any attempt to frame a public philosophy: it simply opted out of the discussion altogether and transferred the most fundamental decisions about life and death to the purely private realm. In the words of Russell Hittinger of Catholic University. *Casey* granted citizens "a private franchise over matters of life and death."

Yesterday that franchise covered abortion; today, assisted suicide; and tomorrow—who knows? The Court has given up any notion that private behavior should be constrained by the public good.

Casey has taken us far beyond the issue of abortion, or even the broader life issues. It has begun to unravel America's civil contract. It is only a short step from here to barbarism.

CHAPTER 4

Affirming Exceptions for Women's Health as Necessary

Case Overview

Stenberg v. Carhart (Carhart I) (2000)

Stenberg v. Carhart (2000) was the first Supreme Court case to focus on a specific abortion procedure. LeRoy Carhart, a Nebraska physician who specialized in reproductive health, challenged a Nebraska state law that prohibited a procedure it termed "partial-birth abortion" and did not provide exceptions to preserve a woman's health. By "partial-birth abortion," the Nebraska law referred to any abortion in which the physician "partially delivers vaginally a living unborn child before killing the unborn child and completing the delivery." Partial-birth abortion is not a medical term; the politically charged term refers to several rare abortion procedures performed during the second trimester. Over 90 percent of all abortions performed in the United States occur during the first trimester.

Carhart brought suit against Don Stenberg, the attorney general of Nebraska, contending that a state law banning certain forms of abortion was unconstitutional based on the undue burden test mentioned by the Court in *Planned Parenthood v. Casey* (1992). Before the U.S. Supreme Court heard the case, both a federal district court and the U.S. court of appeals ruled in support of Carhart. Two issues in particular were brought before the Supreme Court. The first was the lack of an exception for the woman's health, as the State of Nebraska maintained that because certain abortions were never medically necessary a health exception was not needed. The second issue was the vagueness of the statute and whether the language of the law might be construed to apply to other forms of abortion, which would violate the right to privacy supported by the *Roe v. Wade* (1973) and *Casey* decisions.

The Supreme Court struck down the law by a 5-4 majority, finding that the Nebraska statute criminalizing so-called partial birth abortions violated the Due Process Clause of the Constitution, as interpreted in *Planned Parenthood v. Casey* and *Roe v. Wade*. Writing the majority opinion for the Court, Stephen Breyer said that any law that caused women who sought an abortion to "fear prosecution, conviction, and imprisonment" was an undue burden and therefore unconstitutional. John Paul Stevens, David Souter, Sandra Day O'Connor, and Ruth Bader Ginsburg joined the majority, with Ginsburg, O'Connor, and Stevens writing separate concurring opinions. Ginsburg and Stevens asserted that a state could not force a doctor to perform any procedure other than what the doctor felt would be safest. O'Connor agreed that physicians would know best what procedures were medically safest; furthermore, she said, any law that proscribed an abortion procedure needed an exception for the health of the mother.

In his dissent, Clarence Thomas maintained that abortion is not a protected right contained within the Constitution and that "privacy" is not explicitly mentioned in the Constitution. Furthermore, Thomas pointed out, many groups argued that partial-birth abortion was very different from other kinds of abortion and had been considered infanticide. Anthony Kennedy also wrote a dissent, in which he contended that Nebraska's law was allowed under *Planned Parenthood v. Casey*, which allowed that states have a right to protect prenatal life. William Rehnquist and Antonin Scalia also wrote dissents. Scalia stated that the undue burden standard was illegitimate and called for *Casey* to be overruled.

In the aftermath of *Stenberg v. Carhart*, all other state laws banning so-called partial birth abortion were struck down. A few years later, however, Congress passed the Partial-Birth Abortion Ban Act of 2003, and president George W. Bush signed it into federal law.

"The State fails to demonstrate that banning D&X without a health exception may not create significant health risks for women."

Majority Opinion: Physicians and Women Should Make Health Decisions

Stephen Breyer

Stephen Breyer was appointed to the Supreme Court in 1994 by President Bill Clinton. He generally takes a pragmatic approach to constitutional issues and is interested more in producing coherence and continuity in the law than in following doctrinal, historical, or textual strictures.

Breyer wrote and delivered the Court's majority opinion in the case of Stenberg v. Carhart *(2000), excerpted here. In a 5-4 decision, the Court ruled that restrictions on abortions before viability that lack protection for women's health violate* Roe v. Wade *(1973) and other Supreme Court precedents. Breyer states that Nebraska's abortion ban is unconstitutionally broad and vague and unduly burdens a woman's right to choose an abortion. The case confirms that* Roe *and* Planned Parenthood v. Casey *(1992) guaranteed a woman's right to choose the safest abortion method for her circumstances.*

We again consider the right to an abortion. We understand the controversial nature of the problem. Millions of Americans believe that life begins at conception and conse-

Stephen Breyer, majority opinion, *Stenberg v. Carhart*, U.S. Supreme Court, June 28, 2000.

quently that an abortion is akin to causing the death of an innocent child; they recoil at the thought of a law that would permit it. Other millions fear that a law that forbids abortion would condemn many American women to lives that lack dignity, depriving them of equal liberty and leading those with least resources to undergo illegal abortions with the attendant risks of death and suffering. Taking account of these virtually irreconcilable points of view, aware that constitutional law must govern a society whose different members sincerely hold directly opposing views, and considering the matter in light of the Constitution's guarantees of fundamental individual liberty, this Court, in the course of a generation, has determined and then redetermined that the Constitution offers basic protection to the woman's right to choose. We shall not revisit those legal principles. Rather, we apply them to the circumstances of this case.

Three established principles determine the issue before us. We shall set them forth in the language of the joint opinion in *Casey*. First, before "viability . . . the woman has a right to choose to terminate her pregnancy."

Second, "a law designed to further the State's interest in fetal life which imposes an undue burden on the woman's decision before fetal viability" is unconstitutional. An "undue burden is . . . shorthand for the conclusion that a state regulation has the purpose or effect of placing a substantial obstacle in the path of a woman seeking an abortion of a nonviable fetus."

Third, "'subsequent to viability, the State in promoting its interest in the potentiality of human life may, if it chooses, regulate, and even proscribe, abortion except where it is necessary, in appropriate medical judgment, for the preservation of the life or health of the mother.'"

We apply these principles to a Nebraska law banning "partial birth abortion." The statute reads as follows:

"No partial birth abortion shall be performed in this state, unless such procedure is necessary to save the life of the mother whose life is endangered by a physical disorder, physical illness, or physical injury, including a life-endangering physical condition caused by or arising from the pregnancy itself."

The statute defines "partial birth abortion" as:

"an abortion procedure in which the person performing the abortion partially delivers vaginally a living unborn child before killing the unborn child and completing the delivery."

It further defines "partially delivers vaginally a living unborn child before killing the unborn child" to mean

"deliberately and intentionally delivering into the vagina a living unborn child, or a substantial portion thereof, for the purpose of performing a procedure that the person performing such procedure knows will kill the unborn child and does kill the unborn child."

The law classifies violation of the statute as a "Class III felony" carrying a prison term of up to 20 years, and a fine of up to $25,000. It also provides for the automatic revocation of a doctor's license to practice medicine in Nebraska.

We hold that this statute violates the Constitution. . . .

Description of Abortion Procedures

Because Nebraska law seeks to ban one method of aborting a pregnancy, we must describe and then discuss several different abortion procedures. Considering the fact that those procedures seek to terminate a potential human life, our discussion may seem clinically cold or callous to some, perhaps horrifying to others. There is no alternative way, however, to acquaint the reader with the technical distinctions among different abortion methods and related factual matters, upon which the outcome of this case depends. For that reason, drawing upon the findings of the trial court, underlying testimony, and related medical texts, we shall describe the relevant methods of performing abortions in technical detail.

The evidence before the trial court, as supported or supplemented in the literature, indicates the following:

1. About 90% of all abortions performed in the United States take place during the first trimester of pregnancy, before 12 weeks of gestational age. During the first trimester, the predominant abortion method is "vacuum aspiration," which involves insertion of a vacuum tube (cannula) into the uterus to evacuate the contents. Such an abortion is typically performed on an outpatient basis under local anesthesia. Vacuum aspiration is considered particularly safe. The procedure's mortality rates for first trimester abortion are, for example, 5 to 10 times lower than those associated with carrying the fetus to term. Complication rates are also low. As the fetus grows in size, however, the vacuum aspiration method becomes increasingly difficult to use.

2. Approximately 10% of all abortions are performed during the second trimester of pregnancy (12 to 24 weeks). In the early 1970's, reducing labor through the injection of saline into the uterus was the predominant method of second trimester abortion. Today, however, the medical profession has switched from medical induction of labor to surgical procedures for most second trimester abortions. The most commonly used procedure is called "dilation and evacuation" (D&E). That procedure (together with a modified form of vacuum aspiration used in the early second trimester) accounts for about 95% of all abortions performed from 12 to 20 weeks of gestational age.

The Dilation and Extraction Procedure

3. D&E "refers generically to transcervical procedures performed at 13 weeks gestation or later. The American Medical Association Report, adopted by the District Court, describes the process as follows.

Between 13 and 15 weeks of gestation:

"D&E; is similar to vacuum aspiration except that the cervix must be dilated more widely because surgical instruments are used to remove larger pieces of tissue. Osmotic dilators are usually used. Intravenous fluids and an analgesic or sedative may be administered. A local anesthetic such as a paracervical block may be administered, dilating agents, if used, are removed and instruments are inserted through the cervix into the uterus to removal fetal and placental tissue. Because fetal tissue is friable and easily broken, the fetus may not be removed intact. The walls of the uterus are scraped with a curette to ensure that no tissue remains." . . .

5. The D&E procedure carries certain risks. The use of instruments within the uterus creates a danger of accidental perforation and damage to neighboring organs. Sharp fetal bone fragments create similar dangers. And fetal tissue accidentally left behind can cause infection and various other complications. Nonetheless studies show that the risks of mortality and complication that accompany the D&E procedure between the 12th and 20th weeks of gestation are significantly lower than those accompanying induced labor procedures (the next safest midsecond trimester procedures).

6. At trial, Dr. [Leroy] Carhart and Dr. [Phillip] Stubblefield described a variation of the D&E procedure, which they referred to as an "intact D&E." Like other versions of the D&E technique, it begins with induced dilation of the cervix. The procedure then involves removing the fetus from the uterus through the cervix "intact," *i.e.*, in one pass, rather than in several passes. It is used after 16 weeks at the earliest, as vacuum aspiration becomes ineffective and the fetal skull becomes too large to pass through the cervix. The intact D&E proceeds in one of two ways, depending on the presentation of the fetus. If the fetus presents head first (a vertex presentation), the doctor collapses the skull; and the doctor then extracts the entire fetus through the cervix. If the fetus

presents feet first (a breech presentation), the doctor pulls the fetal body through the cervix, collapses the skull, and extracts the fetus through the cervix. The breech extraction version of the intact D&E is also known commonly as "dilation and extraction," or D&X. In the late second trimester, vertex, breech, and traverse/compound (sideways) presentations occur in roughly similar proportions. . . .

No Exceptions Provided

The question before us is whether Nebraska's statute, making criminal the performance of a "partial birth abortion," violates the Federal Constitution, as interpreted in *Planned Parenthood of Southeastern Pa. v. Casey* (1992), and *Roe v. Wade* (1973). We conclude that it does for at least two independent reasons. First, the law lacks any exception "'for the preservation of the . . . health of the mother.'" Second, it "imposes an undue burden on a woman's ability" to choose a D&E abortion, thereby unduly burdening the right to choose abortion itself. We shall discuss each of these reasons in turn.

The *Casey* joint opinion reiterated what the Court held in *Roe*; that "'subsequent to viability, the State in promoting its interest in the potentiality of human life may, if it chooses, regulate, and even proscribe, abortion *except where it is necessary, in appropriate medical judgment, for the preservation of the life or health of the mother.*'" . . .

Nebraska responds that the law does not require a health exception unless there is a need for such an exception. And here there is no such need, it says. It argues that "safe alternatives remain available" and "a ban on partial-birth abortion/D&X would create no risk to the health of women." The problem for Nebraska is that the parties strongly contested this factual question in the trial court below; and the findings and evidence support Dr. Carhart. The State fails to demonstrate that banning D&X without a health exception may not create significant health risks for women, because the record shows that significant medical authority supports the proposition that in some circumstances, D&X would be the safest procedure. . . .

Nebraska's Argument

Nebraska, along with supporting *amici*, replies that these findings are irrelevant, wrong, or applicable only in a tiny number of instances. It says (1) that the D&X procedure is "little-used," (2) by only "a handful of doctors." It argues (3) that D&E and labor induction are at all times "safe alternative procedures." It refers to the testimony of petitioners' medical expert, who testified (4) that the ban would not increase a woman's risk of several rare abortion complications. . . .

The Association of American Physicians and Surgeons et al., *amici* supporting Nebraska, argue (5) that elements of the D&X procedure may create special risks, including cervical incompetence caused by overdilitation, injury caused by conversion of the fetal presentation, and dangers arising from the "blind" use of instrumentation to pierce the fetal skull while lodged in the birth canal.

Nebraska further emphasizes (6) that there are no medical studies "establishing the safety of the partial-birth abortion/D&X procedure," Brief for Petitioners 39, and "no medical studies comparing the safety of partial-birth abortion/D&X to other abortion procedures." It points to (7) an American Medical Association policy statement that "'there does not appear to be any identified situation in which intact D&X is the only appropriate procedure to induce abortion.'" And it points out (8) that the American College of Obstetricians and Gynecologists qualified its statement that D&X "may be the best or most appropriate procedure," by adding that the panel "could identify no circumstances under which [the D&X] procedure . . . would be the only option to save the life or preserve the health of the woman."

The Court's Findings

We find these eight arguments insufficient to demonstrate that Nebraska's law needs no health exception. For one thing, certain of the arguments are beside the point. The D&X procedure's relative rarity (argument (1)) is not highly relevant. The D&X is an infrequently used abortion procedure; but the health exception question is whether protecting women's health requires an exception for those infrequent occasions. A rarely used treatment might be necessary to treat a rarely occurring disease that could strike anyone—the State cannot prohibit a person from obtaining treatment simply by pointing out that most people do not need it. Nor can we know whether the fact that only a "handful" of doctors use the procedure (argument (2)) reflects the comparative rarity of late second term abortions, the procedure's recent development, the controversy surrounding it, or, as Nebraska suggests, the procedure's lack of utility.

For another thing, the record responds to Nebraska's (and *amici*'s) medically based arguments. In respect to argument (3), for example, the District Court agreed that alternatives, such as D&E and induced labor, are "safe" but found that the D&X method was significantly *safer* in certain circumstances. In respect to argument (4), the District Court simply relied on different expert testimony—testimony stating that "'[a]nother advantage of the Intact D&E is that it eliminates the risk of embolism of cerebral tissue into the woman's blood stream.'"

In response to *amici*'s argument (5), the American College of Obstetricians and Gynecologists, in its own *amici* brief, denies that D&X generally poses risks greater than the alternatives. It says that the suggested alternative procedures involve similar or greater risks of cervical and uterine injury, for "D&E procedures, involve similar amounts of dilatation" and "of, course childbirth involves even greater cervical dilitation." The College points out that Dr. Carhart does not reposition the fetus thereby avoiding any risks stemming from conversion to breech presentation, and that, as compared with D&X,

D&E involves the same, if not greater, "blind" use of sharp instruments in the uterine cavity.

We do not quarrel with Nebraska's argument (6), for Nebraska is right. There are no general medical studies documenting comparative safety. Neither do we deny the import of the American Medical Association's statement (argument (7))—even though the State does omit the remainder of that statement: "The AMA recommends that the procedure not be used *unless alternative procedures pose materially greater risk to the woman.*"

Reduced Risk in Some Circumstances

We cannot, however, read the American College of Obstetricians and Gynecologists panel's qualification (that it could not "identify" a circumstance where D&X was the "only" life- or health-preserving option) as if, according to Nebraska's argument (8), it denied the potential health-related need for D&X. That is because the College writes the following in its *amici* brief:

> "Depending on the physician's skill and experience, the D&X procedure can be the most appropriate abortion procedure for some women in some circumstances. D&X presents a variety of potential safety advantages over other abortion procedures used during the same gestational period. . . ."

The upshot is a District Court finding that D&X significantly obviates health risks in certain circumstances, a highly plausible record-based explanation of why that might be so, a division of opinion among some medical experts over whether D&X is generally safer, and an absence of controlled medical studies that would help answer these medical questions. Given these medically related evidentiary circumstances, we believe the law requires a health exception. . . .

The Eighth Circuit found the Nebraska statute unconstitutional because, in *Casey*'s words, it has the "effect of placing a substantial obstacle in the path of a woman seeking an abortion of a nonviable fetus." It thereby places an "undue burden" upon a woman's right to terminate her pregnancy before viability. Nebraska does not deny that the statute imposes an "undue burden" *if* it applies to the more commonly used D&E procedure as well as to D&X. And we agree with the Eighth Circuit that it does so apply. . . .

Even if the statute's basic aim is to ban D&X, its language makes clear that it also covers a much broader category of procedures. The language does not track the medical differences between D&E and D&X—though it would have been a simple matter, for example, to provide an exception for the performance of D&E and other abortion procedures. Nor does the statute anywhere suggest that its application turns on whether a portion of the fetus' body is drawn into the vagina as part of a process to extract an intact fetus after collapsing the head as opposed to a process that would dismember the fetus. Thus, the dissenters' argument that the law was generally intended to bar D&X can be both correct and irrelevant. The relevant question is *not* whether the legislature wanted to ban D&X it is whether the law was intended to apply *only* to D&X. The plain language covers both procedures. . . . Both procedures can involve the introduction of a "substantial portion" of a still living fetus, through the cervix, into the vagina—the very feature of an abortion that leads Justice Thomas to characterize such a procedure as involving "partial birth." . . .

In sum, using this law some present prosecutors and future Attorneys General may choose to pursue physicians who use D&E procedures, the most commonly used method for performing previability second trimester abortions. All those who perform abortion procedures using that method must fear prosecution, conviction, and imprisonment. The result is an undue burden upon a woman's right to make an abortion decision. We must consequently find the statute unconstitutional.

The judgment of the Court of Appeals is *Affirmed.*

> *"Today, the Court inexplicably holds that the States cannot constitutionally prohibit a method of abortion that millions find hard to distinguish from infanticide and that the Court hesitates even to describe."*

Dissenting Opinion: The State Has a Legitimate Interest in Protecting Fetal Life

Clarence Thomas

Clarence Thomas is the second African American to serve on the U.S. Supreme Court. When Thurgood Marshall retired in 1991, President George H.W. Bush nominated Thomas to the Supreme Court. Thomas's nomination met strong opposition from minority groups who opposed Thomas's conservative views on civil rights. Since becoming a justice in 1991, Thomas has aligned closely with the far right of the Court.

In the following dissent, Thomas argues that the standard set by Planned Parenthood v. Casey *(1992) has no precedent and that the Court's decision in* Stenberg v. Carhart, *which struck down as unconstitutional restrictions on abortion before viability that lack exceptions for women's health, is irreconcilable with Casey's undue-burden standards. He calls the Court's ruling in* Carhart *indefensible and illogical, and he argues that the Court's decision is based on misguided personal judicial philosophy rather than historical or doctrinal precedent.*

Clarence Thomas, dissenting opinion, *Stenberg v. Carhart*, U.S. Supreme Court, June 28, 2000.

In 1973, this Court struck down an Act of the Texas Legislature that had been in effect since 1857, thereby rendering unconstitutional abortion statutes in dozens of States. *Roe v. Wade.* As some of my colleagues on the Court, past and present, ably demonstrated, that decision was grievously wrong. Abortion is a unique act, in which a woman's exercise of control over her own body ends, depending on one's view, human life or potential human life. Nothing in our Federal Constitution deprives the people of this country of the right to determine whether the consequences of abortion to the fetus and to society outweigh the burden of an unwanted pregnancy on the mother. Although a State *may* permit abortion, nothing in the Constitution dictates that a State *must* do so.

In the years following *Roe*, this Court applied, and, worse, extended, that decision to strike down numerous state statutes that purportedly threatened a woman's ability to obtain an abortion. The Court voided parental consent laws, legislation requiring that second-trimester abortions take place in hospitals, and even a requirement that both parents of a minor be notified before their child has an abortion. It was only a slight exaggeration when this Court described, in 1976, a right to abortion "without interference from the State." The Court's expansive application of *Roe* in this period, even more than *Roe* itself, was fairly described as the "unrestrained imposition of [the Court's] own, extraconstitutional value preferences" on the American people.

It appeared that this era of Court-mandated abortion on demand had come to an end, first with our decision in *Webster v. Reproductive Health Services*, (1989), and then finally (or so we were told) in our decision in *Planned Parenthood of Southeastern Pa. v. Casey*, (1992). Although in *Casey* the separate opinions of The Chief Justice [William Rehnquist] and Justice [Antonin] Scalia urging the Court to overrule *Roe* did not command a majority, seven Members of that Court, including six Members sitting today, acknowledged that States have a legitimate role in regulating abortion and recognized the States' interest in respecting fetal life at all stages of development. The joint opinion authored by Justices [Sandra Day] O'Connor, [Anthony] Kennedy, and [David] Souter concluded that prior case law "went too far" in "undervalu[ing] the State's interest in potential life" and in "striking down . . . some abortion regulations which in no real sense deprived women of the ultimate decision." *Roe* and subsequent cases, according to the joint opinion, had wrongly "treat[ed] all governmental attempts to influence a woman's decision on behalf of the potential life within her as unwarranted," a treatment that was "incompatible with the recognition that there is a substantial state interest in potential life throughout pregnancy." Accordingly, the joint opinion held that so long as state regulation of abortion furthers legitimate interests—that is, interests not designed to strike at the right itself—the regulation is invalid only if it imposes an undue burden on a woman's ability to obtain an abortion, meaning that it places a *substantial obstacle* in the woman's path.

Court's Position Indefensible

My views on the merits of the *Casey* joint opinion have been fully articulated by others. I will not restate those views here, except to note that the *Casey* joint opinion was constructed by its authors out of whole cloth. The standard set forth in the *Casey* joint opinion has no historical or doctrinal pedigree. The standard is a product of its authors' own philosophical views about abortion, and it should go without saying that it has no origins in or relationship to the Constitution and is, consequently, as illegitimate as the standard it purported to replace. Even assuming, however, as I will for the remainder of this dissent, that *Casey*'s fabricated undue-burden standard merits adherence (which it does not), today's decision is extraordinary. Today, the Court inexplicably holds that the States cannot Constitutionally prohibit a method of abortion that millions find hard to distinguish from infanticide and that the Court hesitates even to describe. This holding cannot be reconciled with *Casey*'s undue-burden standard, as that standard was explained to us by the authors of the joint opinion, and the majority hardly pretends otherwise. In striking down this statute—which expresses a profound and legitimate respect for fetal life and which leaves unimpeded several other safe forms of abortion—the majority opinion gives the lie to the promise of *Casey* that regulations that do no more than "express profound respect for the life of the unborn are permitted, if they are not a substantial obstacle to the woman's exercise of the right to choose" whether or not to have an abortion. Today's decision is so obviously irreconcilable with *Casey*'s explication of what its undue-burden standard requires, let alone the Constitution, that it should be seen for what it is, a reinstitution of the pre-*Webster* abortion-on-demand era in which the mere invocation of "abortion rights" trumps any contrary societal interest. If this statute is unconstitutional under *Casey*, then *Casey* meant nothing at all, and the Court should candidly admit it.

To reach its decision, the majority must take a series of indefensible steps. The majority must first disregard the principles that this Court follows in every context but abortion: We interpret statutes according to their plain meaning and we do not strike down statutes susceptible of a narrowing construction. The majority also must disregard the very constitutional standard it purports to employ, and then displace the considered judgment of the people of Nebraska and 29 other States. The majority's decision is lamentable, because of the result the majority reaches, the illogical steps the majority takes to reach it, and because it portends a return to an era I had thought we had at last abandoned. . . .

We were reassured repeatedly in *Casey* that not all regulations of abortion are unwarranted and that the States may express profound respect for fetal life. Under *Casey*, the regulation before us today should easily pass constitutional muster. But the Court's abortion jurisprudence is a particularly virulent strain of constitutional exegesis. And so today we are told that 30 States are prohibited from banning one rarely used form of abortion that they believe to border on infanticide. It is clear that the Constitution does not compel this result.

I respectfully dissent.

> "While Stenberg *is not, technically, a case about federalism, it provides the Supreme Court with a singular opportunity to take a small step toward more open, decentralized, and competitive politics."*

Stenberg Provides an Important Step Toward the Future of States' Rights

Michael S. Greve

Michael S. Greve cofounded the Center for Individual Rights, a public interest law firm. Also the director of the Federalism Project at the American Enterprise Institute, he has written numerous publications on the American legal system.

> *Greve wrote the following viewpoint shortly before the case of* Stenberg v. Carhart *was decided by the Supreme Court in 2000.* Stenberg *overturned state laws restricting abortions before viability that lack protections for women's health. Greve argues that in addition to being central to the abortion question,* Stenberg *is central to what he calls the Supreme Court's federalism agenda. He notes that the court has become more conservative and has consistently favored states' rights over national laws in its decisions, and he argues that federalism allows for a more democratic process than national consensus.*

Over the last five years [1995–2000], renewing federalism has been the Supreme Court's key project. In its current term, the Court will decide a number of federalism cases. Per-

Michael S. Greve, "Federal Cases," *National Review,* vol. 52, May 1, 2000, pp. 34–36. Copyright © 2000 by National Review, Inc., 215 Lexington Avenue, New York, NY 10016. Reproduced by permission.

haps the most important of them is *Stenberg v. Carhart*. . . . The Court's first major abortion case since *Planned Parenthood v. Casey* in 1992, *Stenberg* will decide whether the *Casey* decision permits states to ban partial-birth abortions.

While *Stenberg* is not, technically, a case about federalism, it provides the Supreme Court with a singular opportunity to take a small but politically significant step toward more open, decentralized, and competitive politics. For this reason, *Stenberg* is central not only to the abortion question but also to the Supreme Court's federalism agenda and to the future of conservative politics. These things are intertwined, and one must hope that the Court will see the connection.

The Court's federalism cases since 1995—virtually all of them decided by a bare 5-4 majority of conservative and centrist justices—hew to a distinct pattern. First, the Court's federalism tends to benefit state and local governments, rather than citizens. For example, the Court has granted state governments—but not private employers—exemptions from damage lawsuits under certain federal labor laws. Second, with one arguable exception (*City of Boerne v. Flores*, the 1997 decision that invalidated the Religious Freedom Restoration Act), the Court has been federalist on issues of marginal political significance, such as the Gun Free School Zones Act, struck down in *United States v. Lopez* (1995). Third, the Court has tended to concentrate its fire on congressional overreaching, not on previous erosions of federalism by the Court itself.

Advancing Federalism

These decisions have advanced federalism in an incremental fashion. If the Court is serious about federalist principles, however, it must assert them on an issue that really matters to citizens. Moreover, the Court must follow its federalist instincts even—indeed, especially—when the national imposition at issue is the fault of the Court rather than the Congress.

Abortion on demand is, of course, the most glaring example of such an imposition. Partial-birth-abortion bans have been enacted in over half the states (in at least four states, over the governor's veto). Yet, following the tenor (if not the holdings) of *Roe* and *Casey*, federal courts have invalidated virtually all those bans. The time has come for the Supreme Court to recognize that this ruthless nationalism is threatening its own federalism agenda.

For all the folklore about the Court as the guardian of liberty and the Court's own counter-majoritarian bluster, the justices cannot for any length of time enforce constitutional norms against the will of the country and without a political base of support. The Court learned that lesson in 1937, when it had to surrender federalism (among other constitutional principles) to the New Deal's nationalist aspirations.

The modern Supreme Court's federalism is encountering a lot of powerful enemies—and very few friends. Liberal elites and constituencies are reflexively nationalist. Business interests favor a national arena, for a number of economic reasons. Congressmen and senators of both parties cheerfully vote for further extensions of federal authority, often near unanimously (witness the proliferation of federal crimes, which now include the impersonation of a 4-H member). The only substantial force for federalism is the conservative movement—including, prominently, the right-to-life constituency that is hoping for a favorable decision in *Stenberg*.

Strengthening States' Rights

In this key case, a decision permitting some state regulation of abortion would resound well beyond abortion politics—because more decentralized, federalist politics would result in more conservative politics pretty much across the board. For one thing, most states are more conservative than Washington, D.C. Over 30 states have acceded to the National Rifle Association's [NRA] most "extreme" demand and authorized concealed-weapons permits; in Washington, meanwhile, the NRA is playing permanent defense.

Decentralized politics also favor conservatives because they are more experimental and competitive. They allow conservatives to show that their experiments work, in due course leading citizens to embrace those experiments. (School choice is a perfect example.) In contrast, liberal experiments usually involve robbing Peter to pay Paul; and the citizens and businesses receiving the short end of the stick tend to vote with their feet and move to more hospitable jurisdictions. Liberals can win only by inducing Washington, D.C., to cut off the exit routes. For all these reasons, conservative constituencies have a huge stake in *Stenberg*'s promise of a more decentralized, federalist Constitution.

Alas, Justices [Anthony] Kennedy and [Sandra Day] O'Connor, whose votes decide federalism cases, do not like federalism's conservative constituencies. Delighted to discuss the finer points of federalism with a bipartisan coalition of respectable governors, they recoil when federalism might give more running room to uncouth Catholics who wave placards of dismembered babies.

Justice Kennedy in particular has amply demonstrated his distaste for conservative reform projects. Generally a staunch federalist, Kennedy helped overturn conservative state referenda on term limits and gay rights. His firmest endorsement of federalism came in *City of Boerne*—a defeat for religious conservatives. While conservatives muted their criticism of the result in *Boerne* precisely because it was reached on federalism grounds, a judicial slap at conservatives in *Stenberg* might well eviscerate all political support for the Supreme Court's federalism.

To illustrate, it helps to think ahead to a possible case involving a federal ban on partial-birth abortions. Having twice come close to overriding President [Bill] Clinton's veto of such legislation, Congress is trying again. The House passed the ban for a third time in April [2000] and an adverse ruling in *Stenberg* would surely add momentum to the legislative effort. Under the Supreme Court's federalism precedents, though, neither the commerce clause nor the Fourteenth Amendment (nor any other constitutional provision) provides a basis for congressional legislation.

So the Supreme Court would probably be right to invalidate such a federal statute. Were such a decision to come after a judicial ruling in *Stenberg* that states may regulate (some) abortions, it would be a clever way of advancing federalism. Liberals would cheer the pro-choice result and grumble about the reasoning; conservatives would do the reverse. Neither side would mobilize seriously to overturn the decision; both would take the fight to the states.

In contrast, consecutive decisions to the effect that neither the states nor the Congress may regulate even the most gruesome abortion procedures would signal that the Supreme Court's commitment isn't to federalism but to judicial supremacy.

Federalism means that citizens in some states will, in the process of governing themselves, offend Barbra Streisand's [singer/actress known for liberal political activism] sensibilities. The Supreme Court must be prepared to tolerate such openness—or else, forget about federalism.

The Supreme Court's federalism is facing an uncertain future. Let a future President . . . replace a single conservative or moderate justice, and federalism—along with school choice and government neutrality in matters of race—will turn from realistic expectation to constitutional corpse. (Abortion on demand will be enshrined for decades.) If constitutional federalism is to have a future, [George W.] Bush must win [the 2000 election]. The federalist justices, though, must do their part. They must realize that *Stenberg* is central to federalism's future—and decide accordingly.

"Stenberg *constitutionalized a right to violence, a right to harm another human being in the most gruesome way imaginable.*"

Stenberg Disregards the Life of the Fetus

Michael Scaperlanda and John Breen

Michael Scaperlanda is the Gene and Elaine Edwards Family Chair and Professor, University of Oklahoma College of Law. John Breen is an associate professor at Loyola University Chicago School of Law.

In the following viewpoint, Scaperlanda and Breen maintain that in Stenberg v. Carhart, *which struck down as unconstitutional state laws that restrict abortion if they fail to protect the woman's health, the exception for health of the woman is so broad that it permits abortion in almost any circumstance. They also argue that the Court is hypocritical in recognizing the human dignity of a violent criminal, as in the death penalty case of* Furman v. Georgia *(1972), while refusing to acknowledge the human dignity of an "innocent child struggling to be born."*

At the beginning of his majority opinion in *Stenberg* [*v. Carhart*, (2000)]. Justice Stephen Breyer notes that the act of abortion can be described in disparate ways. He acknowledges that some people believe that the abortion license is necessary to ensure the "equal liberty" of American women,

Michael Scaperlanda and John Breen, "Never Get Out'a the Boat: *Stenberg v. Carhart* and the Future of American Law," *bepress Legal Series*, Working Paper 1118, March 11, 2006, pp. 1–35. Copyright © 2006 by Michael Scaperlanda and John Breen. Reproduced by permission of the authors.

while others hold that "an abortion is akin to causing the death of an innocent child." Even here, however, Breyer finds it difficult to state the pro-life position in unvarnished form. Opponents of abortion do not believe that the act is merely *akin* to causing the death of an innocent child but that it *is* the deliberate and intentional killing of an innocent child. Regardless of the specific articulation, it seems that for Breyer such description is merely rhetorical gloss. He gives no indication that there is any truth beyond the political preference for or against abortion that would support or refute such a description. There is only the "truth" constructed by the Court according to which abortion is a constitutional right, a right that the Court "has determined and then redetermined" in the course of a generation, first in *Roe v. Wade* [1973] and later in *Planned Parenthood v. Casey* [1992]. Thus, in giving constitutional sanction to partial birth abortion, the *Stenberg* court does not bother to deny that the subject of this gruesome procedure is in fact a human life, a human being, a child in the process of being born. Indeed the unspoken premise upon which the *Stenberg* decision turns is that the humanity or inhumanity of the entity aborted is irrelevant to the constitutionality of the act. . . .

In 2003, Congress passed and President [George W.] Bush signed a federal ban on partial birth abortion. The statute was immediately challenged by advocates of the procedure in three federal actions filed in New York, San Francisco and Omaha. The district court in each of these lawsuits ruled that the federal statute, like its state counterparts, violated the constitutional freedom set forth in *Stenberg*. The Second, Eighth, and Ninth Circuit Courts of Appeal have in turn affirmed each of these respective decisions. To date, every court to consider the matter found that the statute was deficient because it lacked a "health" exception that would allow the procedure where, in the language of *Casey*, it was deemed "necessary, in appropriate medical judgment for the preservation of the life or health of the mother." Although these words sound like words of limitation, from the beginning of its abortion jurisprudence, the Court has given the term "health" an exceedingly broad reading. Indeed, in *Doe v. Bolton*, the companion case to *Roe*, the Court defined "health" to mean "all factors—physical, emotional, psychological, familial, and the woman's age— relevant to the well-being of the patient."

It is this nearly boundless understanding of "health" coupled with a woman's inviolable desire to obtain an abortion that allows the Court to go "all the way." Indeed, it mandates the result in *Stenberg*. Thus, it is hard to take issue with Justice Antonin Scalia's conclusion that *Stenberg* is not "a regrettable misapplication of *Casey*" but the "logical and entirely predictable consequence" of that decision.

An Uncivilized Procedure

Notwithstanding the rhetoric of "health" and the *Stenberg* court's calculated efforts to understate the sheer horror of what it approves, some people can still read a map. . . . After reviewing all the evidence in the New York lawsuit challenging the federal statute. District Judge Richard Casey concluded that partial birth abortion "is a gruesome, brutal, barbaric, and uncivilized medical procedure."

Recognition of this fact would cause most people to run out of the jungle and climb back on board the boat as fast as they can. But "health" gets in the way. . . . In the bizarre world created by *Stenberg*, the Constitution demands that the state not interfere with the "gruesome, brutal, barbaric, and uncivilized" acts that are "necessary" to kill a child in the process of being born. After all, the emotional, psychological, or familial "well-being" of a woman may dictate that she be able to choose the method of her child's execution. She may wish to be reassured that her baby will die quickly and without pain, or that her abortion will be conducted in such as way as to eliminate the possibility of a live birth, or simply in order to please the doctor whom she trusts, the doctor who simply wants to avoid any "unnecessary complications." The point is that "well-being" is broad enough to encompass all of these sorts of considerations, as well as countless others. As such, "health" is no longer firmly rooted in medical science. It is now a word that artfully conceals the exercise of power "without judgment, without judgment." . . .

There is no constitutional provision that expressly guarantees the right to abortion, yet the Court has fashioned a right that far exceeds the boundaries of express guarantee of free speech. Indeed, *Stenberg* constitutionalized a right to violence, a right to harm another human being in the most gruesome way imaginable. In its First Amendment jurisprudence, the Court permits the state to curtail speech because of the state's even more basic interest in curtailing the possibility of violence. The violence in partial birth abortion is no mere possibility. It is a deadly certainty. Nevertheless in *Stenberg* the Court held that the state may not act to prevent the extermination of a human life, a human being, a child in the process of being born, all in the name of freedom.

Abandoning Ordered Liberty

The Court is able to ignore this violence because, in the case of abortion, it has abandoned the idea of ordered liberty in favor of a maximal conception of human freedom. As the Court noted in *Wisconsin v. Yoder* [1972], "the very concept of ordered liberty precludes allowing every person to make his own standards on matters of conduct in which society as a whole has important interests." Yet this is precisely the kind of liberty—the freedom to make one's own standards on matters of life and death, the freedom to kill a child in the process of being born—that the Court embraces in *Stenberg*. Although this understanding of freedom can be found throughout the Court's abortion jurisprudence, it is most clearly stated in *Casey's* now famous mystery passage: "At the heart of liberty is the right to define one's own concept of existence, of meaning, of the universe, and of the mystery of human life." Although much maligned by those critical of the result in *Casey*, the passage is not without some merit. A society that values freedom will not want its government to supply *all* of the answers to life's questions. Indeed, a free society will, within the bounds of ordered liberty, welcome a plurality of responses to the question of value, the question of what kind of life is truly worth living.

At the same time, the freedom to define the "mystery of human life" celebrated in *Casey* cannot include the facts of human life, and ordered liberty does not require the government to remain silent and inactive with respect to these facts. The scientific fact of when human life begins—when *a* human life begins—has not been in doubt since the advent of the modern study of human reproduction. As Keith L. Moore succinctly states in his standard medical text on embryology: "Development begins at fertilization when a sperm fuses with an ovum to form a zygote . . . The zygote is the first cell of a new human being." . . .

Justice Harry Blackmun, the author of *Roe*, recognized that neither the American public nor the logic of American law would accept an opinion that, on the one hand, recognized the humanity of the unborn child and, on the other hand, the right to kill such a human being. . . .

Court Hypocritical in *Roe*

Despite the felt need to provide a seemingly comprehensive history of abortion from antiquity to the present in an opinion exceeding fifty pages, Blackmun was content to make a single, oblique reference to "the well-known facts of fetal development" without elaboration. These facts, it seems, were so well-known they could safely be ignored.

Having established the existence of a dispute, at least rhetorically, it then suited Blackmun's purposes to declare the matter insoluble: "We need not resolve the difficult question of when life begins. When those trained in the respective disciplines of medicine, philosophy, and theology are unable to arrive at any consensus, the judiciary, at this point in the development of man's knowledge, is not in a position to speculate as to the answer." Of course, it would not have been necessary "to speculate as to the answer" of when human life begins had the Court bothered to consult "those trained in the . . . discipline[] of medicine." The Court failed to do precisely that. Instead, Blackmun's only reference to the medical profession is a skewed history of the American Medical Association's [AMA] policy with respect to the permissibility of abortion. That is, Blackmun notes that the AMA adopted a policy favoring restrictive abortion laws in 1857 in order to protect "the independent and actual existence of the child before birth, as a living being" and that the AMA revised its policy in 1970 in response to certain "changes in state laws and by the judicial decisions which tend to make abortion more freely available." Blackmun fails to note, however, that during the intervening period there was no change in the medical conclusion that the victim of abortion is a living human being. The only change in judgment was political in nature, not medical.

Confronting a question which he insisted did not have an answer, Blackmun could then assume a posture of judicial modesty. Indeed, by not speculating as to "this most sensitive and difficult question" he could portray the Court as exercising restraint in the service of freedom. The state, said Blackmun, could not restrict the pregnant woman's freedom of choice "by adopting one theory of life." . . .

Fetal Life Established

There is, of course, nothing *modest* in pretending that science has not resolved the answer to a particular scientific question when in fact it has. And there is nothing *restrained* in ignoring the conclusions of the medical profession that represent the exercise of medical judgment simply in order to reach a particular result. There is, however, something plainly *ludicrous* in suggesting that judge can decide a case without judging. . . . [T]he Court's prohibition against adopting a "theory of life" constitutes a judgment—a judgment that human life worthy of protection begins only after birth, a judgment that under the Constitution one member of the human family may be violently sacrificed at the altar of autonomy in order to vindicate the "dignity" of another.

In declaring that the state must, as a constitutional matter, ignore the humanity of the victim subject to abortion, the Court in *Roe* abandoned both the principle of equal concern and respect and the principle of ordered liberty in favor of the idea of liberty as license. This license, as *Casey* said, includes "the right to define one's own concept of existence, of meaning, of the universe, and the mystery of human life," even if the process of self-definition entails extinguishing the life of another. *Stenberg* lays bare the full implications of this license. The *Stenberg* court does not trouble itself with *Roe*'s fatuous claim that it "need not resolve the difficult question of when life begins." The majority *knows* that the life at issue in the case has already begun. Indeed, *it is in the process of being born*. By embracing what it believes is a maximal conception of human freedom, the Court licenses the brutal killing of what is undeniably an innocent human being. . . .

Accordingly, *Stenberg* makes apparent, as never before, the absurd contradiction that the Court has placed at the foundation of our legal system. . . .

Beyond irony, it is absurd that our law acknowledges the "common human dignity" of a violent criminal [in the death penalty case of *Furman v. Georgia* (1972)] but refuses to recognize this same dignity in an innocent child struggling to be born.

This absurdity is even more pronounced when the holding in *Stenberg* is juxtaposed with the panoply of federal and state efforts intended to extend the protection of law to unborn children, to acknowledge them as members of the human family. It is absurd for the law to make available to grieving parents a cause of action for wrongful death and loss of society for the "death" of an unborn child caused by the negligence of another when the Supreme Court has declared that it cannot resolve the difficult question of when "life" begins. It is absurd for the law to allow for individuals to be prosecuted for homicide for deliberating causing the death of an unborn child when *Roe* and its progeny allow a woman to pay her doctor to deliberately exterminate the same child. If *Stenberg* is correct, if the unborn child has no legal standing up to and including the time of birth, then it is difficult to make sense of federal statutes like the Born-Alive Infants' Protection Act, the Unborn Victims of Violence Act ("Laci and Conner's Law"), and similar measures.

"Nebraska's ban on 'partial-birth abortion' was enacted ... to eviscerate the key protections guaranteed ... by Roe *and* Casey."

Nebraska's Ban on Partial-Birth Abortion Aims to Limit Access to Abortion

Simon Heller et al.

Simon Heller, a staff attorney at the Center for Reproductive Rights, successfully argued Stenberg v. Carhart, *the challenge to Nebraska's ban on so-called partial-birth abortions, before the U.S. Supreme Court in April 2000.*

The following selection is taken from the brief for respondent Dr. LeRoy Carhart et al. in which Simon Heller outlines how the Nebraska law, as written, could apply to all second trimester abortion procedures and outlaw a woman's constitutional right to an abortion.

A woman's right to terminate her pregnancy is firmly rooted in the Constitution, as this Court recognized in *Roe v. Wade* (1973), and *Planned Parenthood v. Casey* (1992). Moreover, *Roe's* essential holding that a woman may terminate her pregnancy prior to viability has repeatedly been affirmed by this Court.

The Petitioners ("the State") seek to alter radically these basic tenets. In sweeping language, the Nebraska "partial-birth abortion" ban prohibits most modern abortion techniques

Simon Heller et al., "Brief of Dr. Carhart et al. in Stenberg v. Carhart," *Issues in Law & Medicine*, vol. 16, Summer 2000, pp. 35–67. Reproduced by permission.

without regard to viability of the fetus. Indeed, the term "partial-birth abortion" was specifically designed to overturn *Roe* by luring this Court away from the viability polestar of its abortion jurisprudence. The Act is part of a coordinated national campaign to expand state interests in previable fetal life at the expense of women's health and liberty. It attempts to eviscerate women's privacy rights by making the location of the fetus in the woman's body—not viability—the defining criterion for women's pregnancy choices.

Since *Roe*, legal abortion has had an enormous positive effect on women's health in this Nation, both because of the development of increasingly safe abortion techniques and because the abortion choice has been available to women who would otherwise be forced to carry unwanted high-risk pregnancies to term. It has become increasingly difficult, however, for women to obtain abortions. Physicians, like Respondent [Dr. LeRoy] Carhart, have been forced to work in an exceedingly hostile climate, created not only by private individuals, but also by legislatures that repeatedly enact anti-abortion legislation without regard to women's health or this Court's abortion jurisprudence. The record in this case establishes that the Act is a deceptive maneuver in the campaign to erode women's right to choose abortion.

The Nebraska Ban

The Act bans "partial-birth abortions." It defines this term to mean "an abortion procedure in which the person performing the abortion partially delivers vaginally a living unborn child before killing the child and completing the delivery." The Act further states: "the term partially delivers vaginally a living unborn child before killing the unborn child means deliberately and intentionally delivering into the vagina a living unborn child, or a substantial portion thereof, for the purpose of performing a procedure that the person performing such procedure knows will kill the unborn child and does kill the unborn child."

The Act contains no exception for abortions performed to protect a woman's health, nor an exception for when a particular method or variation is the safest for a particular woman. The Act contains only a limited exception for abortions performed to save a woman's life; it permits such procedures only where "necessary" to save her life and then only if the woman's life is threatened by a physical condition. By contrast, Nebraska's statute prohibiting post-viability abortions contains exceptions for the woman's life or health with no qualifiers, and permits women requiring such abortions to use the safest method.

The penalty for violating the Act is a maximum prison term of 20 years with up to $25,000 in fines. The Act also provides that a physician's medical license may be revoked for performing a prohibited procedure. These penalties far exceed those Nebraska applied to illegal abortions prior to *Roe*. . . .

Carhart's Medical Practice

Respondent Carhart is a retired Air Force Lieutenant Colonel who was on active duty for 21 years. He has been a doctor since 1973 and has practiced in Nebraska since 1978, when he was assigned to the Offutt Air Force Base in Omaha. He served as Chairman of the surgery department at the base, supervising over twenty doctors, including obstetricians and gynecologists.

Dr. Carhart performs abortions from 3 weeks lmp [last menstrual period] to viability. Because no hospitals openly provide abortions in Nebraska, and because he is the only physician in the state who performs abortions past 16 weeks lmp, Dr. Carhart's patients include women whose lives and health are at risk or whose fetuses have severe anomalies. For example, his patients include women with severe renal failure, severe brittle diabetes, and women whose lives are in jeopardy and are referred to him by the University of Nebraska.

In treating his patients. Dr. Carhart chooses the most appropriate abortion method based on contemporary medical standards and evolving safety criteria. In all abortions after 15 weeks, Dr. Carhart attempts to perform a D&X [dilation and extraction] because it poses less risk of both mortality and morbidity than other D&E [dilation and evacuation] procedures.

When D&X Is Used

To perform a D&E up to 20 weeks, Dr. Carhart uses suction or forceps to rupture the membranes. Then, using forceps, Dr. Carhart attempts to draw the pre-viable fetus into the woman's vagina until the fetal skull lodges in the uterine side of the cervical os [opening]. The fetus is typically and technically alive at this point since Dr. Carhart has not taken any step to ensure fetal demise. Dr. Carhart uses ultrasound during all D&E procedures to minimize the possibility of any unnecessary trauma to the woman; thus, he is able to observe the pre-viable fetus and its heartbeat during the procedure. Because he only performs pre-viability abortions, Dr. Carhart knows that every abortion he performs will cause fetal demise.

Dr. Carhart is not always able to remove an intact fetus because, frequently, after the membranes are ruptured, a fetal extremity spontaneously protrudes into the woman's vagina. When this happens, Dr. Carhart grasps the extremity and pulls the fetus through the cervical os. Even when a limb does not spontaneously protrude, the pre-viable fetus sometimes becomes dismembered by the traction of the fetus against the woman's cervical os while Dr. Carhart is drawing it into her vaginal canal. Thus, when dismemberment occurs, it does so while the fetus is partially in the woman's vagina. Dismemberment of the fetus causes fetal demise.

Because the skull is too large to pass safely through the woman's cervical os, Dr. Carhart either compresses the head of the pre-viable fetus with forceps or perforates the skull and uses a suction cannula to remove its contents. Like dismemberment, removing the contents of the skull also eventually causes fetal demise. If the fetus presents itself head first, Dr. Carhart performs the procedure in reverse order by first decompressing the fetal skull while the body of the fetus is in the uterus.

No Expert Testimony Given

The State produced no expert testimony that D&X is not safe: nor did the State produce any evidence that D&X is not an "abortion" procedure. In fact, the only State witness found credible by the district court, Dr. Boehm, supports the Act based on his understanding that it bans only the D&X technique, and then solely for political and personal reasons—not because the D&X technique is unsafe. In fact, he conceded that D&X could well be safer than other D&E variants. He also admitted that he was not as much of an expert on advances in the D&E procedure, since he has not performed such procedures in the past 10 to 15 years, and that his idea that "partial-birth abortion" is the equivalent of D&X was gained from "the press," a source he would not ordinarily rely upon for formation of his medical opinions.

Moreover, Dr. Boehm testified that without the "substantial portion" language, the Act would prohibit most D&E procedures. Though he testified that the phrase "substantial portion" means "a significant portion of the fetus," he admitted this "definition" was only his "own personal view and not necessarily the view of someone who wants to prosecute this letter of the law." He further admitted that some people may interpret a "substantial portion" to mean a hand or leg and, given that interpretation, the Act proscribes the D&E procedure.

History of the Proceedings

On June 12, 1997, Dr. Carhart filed a complaint challenging the Act's constitutionality in the United States District Court for the District of Nebraska. On July 2, 1998, the district court issued a preliminary injunction against enforcement of the Act as applied to Dr. Carhart and his patients. On August 10, 1998, a final judgment was entered against the defendants permanently enjoining them from enforcing the Act against Dr. Carhart, his patients, and others similarly situated. The district court held that the Act was broad enough to encompass all D&E abortions, and therefore imposed an undue burden; but that, even if it prohibited only certain D&X variants of the D&E, it banned abortion procedures that are the safest for some women and is therefore unconstitutional for this reason as well. The district court further held that the term "substantial portion," essential to understanding the Act's scope, was void for vagueness. The court of appeals affirmed unanimously, upholding all the district court's finding of facts, but reaching only the holding that the Act prohibits all D&Es and therefore imposes an undue burden.

Campaign to Dismantle Abortion Rights

Nebraska's ban on "partial-birth abortion" was enacted as part of a deceptive nationwide campaign to eviscerate the key protections guaranteed to American women by *Roe* and *Casey*. Contrary to the way the State characterizes the Act, its prohibitions are limited neither to one medical procedure nor to post-viability abortions. Rather, any reasonable construction of the plain language of the Act, underscored by its legislative history, establishes that the ban is so broad as to prohibit, at a minimum, the D&E method of abortion, the most common second-trimester abortion method, as both courts below found. Such a broad ban on a safe and common method of abortion performed pre-viability is unconstitutional under the settled precedents of this Court.

Moreover, the Act is not reasonably susceptible to a construction that would limit it to any one well-defined abortion technique: any such construction would require unconstitutional rewriting of the Act and would conflict with the Act's legislative history. Nor would the State's proposed narrowing of the Act to ban only D&X abortions save it. Such a narrower ban would itself be invalid for three reasons. First, it would deprive women of their right to bodily integrity by forcing them to undergo undesired and unnecessary medical procedures and depriving them of access to the method of abortion that would be the safest in their own individual circumstances. Pregnant women seeking abortions should not be forced to endure such physically intrusive alterations in the medical procedures they are to undergo. These are intrusions no other group of persons would ever be expected to endure. Second, the narrower ban would have the effect of imposing an undue burden on women seeking pre-viability abortions because it would harm women's health without serving any legitimate state interest. In addition, it would have the impermissible purpose of according legal protection to the pre-viable fetus based on its location in the woman's body and at the expense of women's health and liberty. Third, it would be unconstitutional because it lacks any exception for women who require abortions to preserve their health, and contains only a grossly inadequate life exception.

Finally, the Act is void for vagueness. By using vague terms such as "substantial portion," the Act fails to give physicians notice of the conduct it prohibits and is an open invitation to arbitrary and discriminatory enforcement. Thus, it will chill the performance of all abortions.

CHAPTER 5

Upholding the Partial-Birth Abortion Ban Act of 2003

Case Overview

Gonzales v. Carhart (Carhart II) (2007)

On November 5, 2003, after it was passed by Congress, President George W. Bush signed the Partial-Birth Abortion Ban Act into federal law. The new law was immediately found unconstitutional in three U.S. district courts: in California, New York, and Nebraska. The U.S. court of appeals found that the government did not provide any additional information that was any different from that of the *Stenberg v. Carhart* (2000) case and ruled that the new federal law was unconstitutional because it did not include an exception for the health of the woman. U.S. attorney general Alberto Gonzales petitioned the U.S. Supreme Court to review the challenges to the Partial-Birth Abortion Ban Act of 2003.

The Supreme Court ruled to reverse the decision of the lower courts. The Court held that the Partial-Birth Abortion Ban Act of 2003 was constitutional and did not impose an undue burden on the due process right of women to obtain an abortion. Writing for the Court's 5-4 majority opinion, Anthony Kennedy, joined by John Roberts, Samuel Alito, Clarence Thomas, and Antonin Scalia, stated that the attorneys for LeRoy Carhart and Planned Parenthood had failed to demonstrate that either the Partial-Birth Abortion Ban Act of 2003 was so broad as to impose an undue burden on a woman's right to an abortion or that Congress lacked the authority to institute a federal ban on a particular medical procedure.

The Court held that lower courts had repudiated the premise of *Planned Parenthood v. Casey* (1992)—that the state had some interest in preserving fetal life. Referencing congressional findings that the medical procedure known as intact dilation and extraction (D&E) is never needed to preserve a woman's health, Kennedy concluded that a health exception was unnecessary. Furthermore, the Court maintained, Congress was authorized to regulate areas of medical disagreement. In its ruling, the Court stated that "ethical and moral concerns" could provide a basis for state and federal legislation about abortion, even before the fetus was viable, or able to survive outside the womb. In a concurring opinion, Clarence Thomas and Antonin Scalia reiterated that in their opinion, the right to abortion "has no basis in the Constitution." They criticized the majority opinion for not explicitly saying that *Roe v. Wade* (1973) had been wrongly decided.

Four justices dissented—Ruth Bader Ginsburg, Stephen Breyer, David Souter, and John Paul Stevens. In the dissent, Ginsburg argued that the Court's ruling was "alarming" in that it ignored *stare decisis*, or the Court's precedent of decision making in abortion cases. Ginsburg maintained that women's right to abortion was grounded in concepts of personal autonomy and equal citizenship as much as the right to privacy granted in the Constitution. She lamented the lack of a health exception in the federal law and noted, "The Court's hostility to the right *Roe* and *Casey* secured is not concealed."

Gonzales v. Carhart opened the door for states to enact restrictive abortion laws without health exceptions and with the expectation that the courts will uphold them.

> *"If some procedures have different risks*
> *than others, it does not follow that the*
> *State is altogether barred from impos-*
> *ing reasonable regulations."*

Majority Opinion: The State's Interest in Promoting Life Justifies Restricting Access to Abortion

Anthony Kennedy

Anthony Kennedy was appointed to the Supreme Court in 1988 by President Ronald Reagan. A generally conservative justice, Kennedy acts as the Court's swing vote on social issues in some cases and has consequently held special prominence in some po- litically charged 5-4 decisions.

In the following 5-4 decision written by Kennedy, the Court upheld the first federal ban on abortion, the Partial-Birth Abor- tion Ban Act of 2003, in Gonzales v. Carhart *(2007). The act had been challenged by lower courts, but the Supreme Court de- termined that it was neither vague nor overbroad and that it provided an adequate exception for the life of the woman.*

The [Partial-Birth Abortion Ban] Act's purposes are set forth in recitals preceding its operative provisions. A de- scription of the prohibited abortion procedure demonstrates the rationale for the congressional enactment. The Act pro- scribes a method of abortion in which a fetus is killed just inches before completion of the birth process. Congress stated

Anthony Kennedy, majority opinion, *Gonzales v. Carhart*, U.S. Supreme Court, April 18, 2007.

as follows: "Implicitly approving such a brutal and inhumane procedure by choosing not to prohibit it will further coarsen society to the humanity of not only newborns, but all vulnerable and innocent human life, making it increasingly difficult to protect such life." The Act expresses respect for the dignity of human life.

Congress was concerned, furthermore, with the effects on the medical community and on its reputation caused by the practice of partial-birth abortion. The findings in the Act explain:

> "Partial-birth abortion . . . confuses the medical, legal, and ethical duties of physicians to preserve and promote life, as the physician acts directly against the physical life of a child, whom he or she had just delivered, all but the head, out of the womb, in order to end that life."

There can be no doubt the government "has an interest in protecting the integrity and ethics of the medical profession." Under our precedents it is clear the State has a significant role to play in regulating the medical profession.

Casey [*Planned Parenthood v. Casey* (1992)] reaffirmed these governmental objectives. The government may use its voice and its regulatory authority to show its profound and respect for the life within the woman. A central premise of the opinion was that the court's precedents after *Roe* [*v. Wade* (1973)] had "undervalue[d] the State's interest in potential life." The plurality opinion indicated "[t]he fact that a law which serves a valid purpose, one not designed to strike at the right itself, has the incidental effect of making it more difficult or more expensive to procure an abortion cannot be enough to invalidate it." This was not an idle assertion. The three premises of *Casey* must coexist. The third premise, that the State, from the inception of the pregnancy, maintains its own regulatory interest in protecting the life of the fetus that may become a child, cannot be set at naught by interpreting *Casey*'s requirement of a health exception so it becomes tantamount to allowing a doctor to choose the abortion method he or she might prefer. Where it has a rational basis to act, and it does not impose an undue burden, the State may use its regulatory power to bar certain procedures and substitute others, all in furtherance of its legitimate interests in regulating the medical profession in order to promote respect for life, including life of the unborn.

Ethical and Moral Concerns

The Act's ban on abortions that involve partial delivery of a living fetus furthers the Government's objectives. No one would dispute that, for many, D&E is a procedure itself laden with the power to devalue human life. Congress could nonetheless conclude that the type of abortion proscribed by the Act requires specific regulation because it implicates additional ethical and moral concerns that justify a special prohibition. Congress determined that the abortion methods it proscribed had a "disturbing similarity to the killing of a newborn infant," and thus it was concerned with "draw[ing] a bright line that clearly distinguished abortion and infanticide." The Court has in the past confirmed the validity of drawing boundaries to prevent certain practices that extinguish life and are close to actions that are condemned. [*Washington v. Glucksberg* (1997)] found reasonable the State's "fear that permitting assisted suicide will start it down the path to voluntary and perhaps even involuntary euthanasia."

Respect for human life finds an ultimate expression in the bond of love the mother has for her child. The Act recognizes this reality as well. Whether to have an abortion requires a difficult and painful moral decision. While we find no reliable data to measure the phenomenon, it seems unexceptionable to conclude some women come to regret their choice to abort the infant life they once created and sustained. Severe depression and loss of esteem can follow.

In a decision so fraught with emotional consequence some doctors may prefer not to disclose precise details of the means that will be used, confining themselves to the required statement of risks the procedure entails. From one standpoint this ought not to be surprising. Any number of patients facing imminent surgical procedures would prefer not to hear all details, lest the usual anxiety preceding invasive medical procedures become the more intense. This is likely the case with the abortion procedures here in issue.

Informing Pregnant Women

It is, however, precisely this lack information concerning the way in which the fetus will be killed that is of legitimate concern to the State. The State has an interest in ensuring so grave a choice is well informed. It is self-evident that a mother who comes to regret her choice to abort must struggle with grief more anguished and sorrow more profound when she learns, only after the event, what she once did not know: that she allowed a doctor to pierce the skull and vacuum the fast-developing brain of her unborn child, a child assuming the human form.

It is a reasonable inference that a necessary effect of the regulation and the knowledge it conveys will be to encourage some women to carry the infant to full term, thus reducing the absolute number of late-term abortions. The medical profession, furthermore, may find different and less shocking methods to abort the fetus in the second trimester, thereby accommodating legislative demand. The State's interest in respect for life is advanced by the dialogue that better informs the political and legal systems, the medical profession, expectant mothers, and society as a whole of the consequences that follow from a decision to elect a late-term abortion.

It is objected that the standard D&E is in some respects as brutal, if not more, than the intact D&E, so that the legislation accomplishes little. What we have already said, however, shows ample justification for the regulation. Partial-birth abortion, as defined by the Act, differs from a standard D&E because the former occurs when the fetus is partially outside the mother to the point of one of the Act's anatomical landmarks. It was reasonable for Congress to think that partial-birth abortion, more than standard D&E, "undermines the public's perception of the appropriate role of a physician during the delivery process, and perverts a process during which life is brought into the world." There would be a flaw in this Court's logic, and an irony in its jurisprudence, were we first to conclude a ban on both D&E and intact D&E was overbroad and then to say it is irrational to ban only intact D&E because that does not proscribe both procedures. In sum, we reject the contention that the congressional purpose of the Act was "to place a substantial obstacle in the path of a woman seeking an abortion."

Lack of Medical Consensus

The Act's furtherance of legitimate government interests bears upon, but does not resolve, the next question: whether the Act has the effect of imposing an unconstitutional burden on the abortion right because it does not allow use of the barred procedure where "'necessary, in appropriate medical judgment, for [the] preservation of the . . . health of the mother.'" The prohibition in the Act would be unconstitutional, under precedents we here assume to be controlling, if it "subject[ed] [women] to significant health risks." In *Ayotte* [*v. Planned Parenthood* (2006)] the parties agreed a health exception to the challenged parental-involvement statute was necessary "to avert serious and often irreversible damage to [a pregnant minor's] health." Here, by contrast, whether the Act creates significant health risks for women has been a contested factual question. The evidence presented in the trial courts and before Congress demonstrates both sides have medical support for their position.

Respondents presented evidence that intact D&E may be the safest method of abortion, for reasons similar to those adduced in *Stenberg* [*v. Carhart* (2006)]. Abortion doctors testified, for example, that intact D&E decreases the risk of cervical laceration or uterine perforation because it requires fewer passes into the uterus with surgical instruments and does not require the removal of bony fragments of the dismembered fetus, fragments that may be sharp. Respondents also presented evidence that intact D&E was safer both because it reduces the risks that fetal parts will remain in the uterus and because it takes less time to complete. Respondents, in addition, proffered evidence that intact D&E was safer for women with certain medical conditions or women with fetuses that had certain anomalies.

These contentions were contradicted by other doctors who testified in the District Courts and before Congress. They concluded that the alleged health advantages were based on speculation without scientific studies to support them. They considered D&E always to be a safe alternative.

There is documented medical disagreement whether the Act's prohibition would ever impose significant health risks on women. The three District Courts that considered the Act's constitutionality appeared to be in some disagreement on this central factual question. The District Court for the District of Nebraska concluded "the banned procedure is, sometimes, the safest abortion procedure to preserve the health of women." The District Court for the Northern District of California reached a similar conclusion. The District Court for the Southern District of New York was more skeptical of the purported health benefits of intact D&E. It found the Attorney General's "expert witness reasonably and effectively refuted [the plaintiffs'] proffered bases for the opinion that [intact D&E] has safety advantages over other second-trimester abortion procedures." In addition it did "not believe that many of [the plaintiffs'] purported reasons for why [intact D&E] is medically necessary [were] credible; rather [it found them to be] theoretical or false." The court nonetheless invalidated the Act because it determined "a significant body of medical opinion ... holds that D & E has safety advantages over induction and that [intact D&E] has some safety advantages (however hypothetical and unsubstantiated by scientific evidence) over D & E for some women in some circumstances."

Legislature May Regulate Medical Procedures

The question becomes whether the Act can stand when this medical uncertainty persists. The Court's precedents instruct that the Act can survive this facial attack. The Court has given state and federal legislatures wide discretion to pass legislation in areas where there is medical and scientific uncertainty.

This traditional rule is consistent with *Casey*, which confirms the State's interest in promoting respect for human life at all stages in the pregnancy. Physicians are not entitled to ignore regulations that direct them to use reasonable alternative procedures. The law need not give abortion doctors unfettered choice in the course of their medical practice, nor should it elevate their status above other physicians in the medical community. In *Casey* the controlling opinion held an informed-consent requirement in the abortion context was "no different from a requirement that a doctor give certain specific information about any medical procedure." The opinion stated "the doctor-patient relation here is entitled to the same solicitude it receives in other contexts."

Medical uncertainty does not foreclose the exercise of legislative power in the abortion context any more than it does in other contexts. The medical uncertainty over whether the Act's prohibition creates significant health risks provides a sufficient basis to conclude in this facial attack that the Act does not impose an undue burden.

No Undue Burden Imposed

The conclusion that the Act does not impose an undue burden is supported by other considerations. Alternatives are available to the prohibited procedure. As we have noted, the Act does not proscribe D&E. One District Court found D&E to have extremely low rates of medical complications. Another indicated D&E was "generally the safest method of abortion during the second trimester." In addition the Act's prohibition only applies to the delivery of "a living fetus." If the intact D&E procedure is truly necessary in some circumstances, it appears likely an injection that kills the fetus is an alternative under the Act that allows the doctor to perform the procedure.

The instant cases, then, are different from *Planned Parenthood of Central Mo. v. Danforth* (1976), in which the Court invalidated a ban on saline amniocentesis, the then-dominant second-trimester abortion method. The Court found the ban in *Danforth* to be "an unreasonable or arbitrary regulation designed to inhibit, and having the effect of inhibiting, the vast majority of abortions after the first 12 weeks." Here the Act allows, among other means, a commonly used and generally accepted method, so it does not construct a substantial obstacle to the abortion right.

In reaching the conclusion the Act does not require a health exception we reject certain arguments made by the parties on both sides of these cases. On the one hand, the Attorney General urges us to uphold the Act on the basis of the congressional findings alone. Although we review congressional factfinding under a deferential standard, we do not in the circumstances here place dispositive weight on Congress' findings. The Court retains an independent institutional duty to review factual findings where constitutional rights are at stake.

Act Is Still Valid

As respondents have noted, and the District Courts recognized, some recitations in the Act are factually incorrect. Whether or not accurate at the time, some of the important findings have been superseded. Two examples suffice. Congress determined no medical schools provide instruction on the prohibited procedure. The testimony in the District Courts, however, demonstrated intact D&E is taught at medical schools. Congress also found there existed a medical consensus that the prohibited procedure is never medically necessary.

On the other hand, relying on the Court's opinion in *Stenberg*, respondents contend that an abortion regulation must contain a health exception "if 'substantial medical authority supports the proposition that banning a particular procedure could endanger women's health.'" As illustrated by respondents' arguments and the decisions of the Courts of Appeals, *Stenberg* has been interpreted to leave no margin of error for legislatures to act in the face of medical uncertainty.

A zero tolerance policy would strike down legitimate abortion regulations, like the present one, if some part of the medical community were disinclined to follow the proscription. This is too exacting a standard to impose on the legislative power, exercised in this instance under the Commerce Clause, to regulate the medical profession. Considerations of marginal safety, including the balance of risks, are within the legislative competence when the regulation is rational and in pursuit of legitimate ends. When standard medical options are available, mere convenience does not suffice to displace them; and if some procedures have different risks than others, it does not follow that the State is altogether barred from imposing reasonable regulations. The Act is not invalid on its face where there is uncertainty over whether the barred procedure is ever necessary to preserve a woman's health, given the availability of other abortion procedures that are considered to be safe alternatives.

Health Exception Unnecessary

The considerations we have discussed support our further determination that these facial attacks should not have been entertained in the first instance. In these circumstances the proper means to consider exceptions is by as-applied challenge. The Government has acknowledged that preenforcement, as-applied challenges to the Act can be maintained. This is the proper manner to protect the health of the woman if it can be shown that in discrete and well-defined instances a particular condition has or is likely to occur in which the procedure prohibited by the Act must be used. In an as-applied challenge the nature of the medical risk can be better quantified and balanced than in a facial attack.

The latitude given facial challenges in the First Amendment context is inapplicable here. Broad challenges of this type impose "a heavy burden" upon the parties maintaining the suit. What that burden consists of in the specific context of abortion statutes has been a subject of some question. We need not resolve that debate.

As the previous sections of this opinion explain, respondents have not demonstrated that the Act would be unconstitutional in a large fraction of relevant cases. We note that the statute here applies to all instances in which the doctor proposes to use the prohibited procedure, not merely those in which the woman suffers from medical complications. It is neither our obligation nor within our traditional institutional role to resolve questions of constitutionality with respect to each potential situation that might develop.

The Act is open to a proper as-applied challenge in a discreet case. No as-applied challenge need be brought if the prohibition in the Act threatens a woman's life because the Act already contains a life exception.

Respondents have not demonstrated that the Act, as a facial matter, is void for vagueness, or that it imposes an undue burden on a woman's right to abortion based on its overbreadth or lack of a health exception. For these reasons the judgments of the Courts of Appeals for the Eighth and Ninth Circuits are reversed.

> "[The majority opinion] reflects ancient notions about women's place in the family and under the Constitution— ideas that have long since been discredited."

Dissenting Opinion: As Equal Citizens, Women Must Control Their Reproductive Lives

Ruth Bader Ginsburg

Ruth Bader Ginsburg was appointed to the Supreme Court in 1993 by President Bill Clinton. She is the second female justice and the first Jewish woman to serve on the Supreme Court. A strong advocate of women's rights, Ginsburg had earlier worked for the American Civil Liberties Union in several capacities.

In her dissent in Gonzales v. Carhart *(2007), Ginsburg denounces the Court's ruling as "alarming," arguing that the Court has undermined* Roe v. Wade *(1973) by supporting an abortion prohibition with no exception safeguarding a woman's health. Ginsburg writes that women's ability to realize their full potential is intimately connected to their ability to control their reproductive lives. She concludes that the Partial-Birth Abortion Act of 2003 and the Court's defense of it cannot be understood as anything other than an effort to chip away at abortion rights.*

Today's decision is alarming. It refuses to take *Casey* [*Planned Parenthood v. Casey* (1992)] and *Stenberg* [*v. Carhart* (2000)] seriously. It tolerates, indeed applauds, federal

Ruth Bader Ginsburg, dissenting opinion, *Gonzales v. Carhart*, U.S. Supreme Court, April 18, 2007.

intervention to ban nationwide a procedure found necessary and proper in certain cases by the American College of Obstetricians and Gynecologists (ACOG). It blurs the line, firmly drawn in *Casey*, between previability and postviability abortions. And, for the first time since *Roe* [*v. Wade* (1973)], the Court blesses a prohibition with no exception safeguarding a woman's health.

I dissent from the Court's disposition. Retreating from prior rulings that abortion restrictions cannot be imposed absent an exception safeguarding a woman's health, the Court upholds an Act that surely would not survive under the close scrutiny that previously attended state-decreed limitations on a woman's reproductive choices.

As *Casey* comprehended, at stake in cases challenging abortion restrictions is a woman's "control over her [own] destiny." "There was a time, not so long ago," when women were "regarded as the center of home and family life, with attendant special responsibilities that precluded full and independent legal status under the Constitution." Those views, this Court made clear in *Casey*, "are no longer consistent with our understanding of the family, the individual, or the Constitution." Women, it is now acknowledged, have the talent, capacity, and right "to participate equally in the economic and social life of the Nation." Their ability to realize their full potential, the Court recognized, is intimately connected to "their ability to control their reproductive lives." Thus, legal challenges to undue restrictions on abortion procedures do not seek to vindicate some generalized notion of privacy; rather, they center on a woman's autonomy to determine her life's course, and thus to enjoy equal citizenship stature.

Safeguarding Women's Health

In keeping with this comprehension of the right to reproductive choice, the Court has consistently required that laws regulating abortion, at any stage of pregnancy and in all cases, safeguard a woman's health.

... In *Stenberg*, we expressly held that a statute banning intact D&E was unconstitutional in part because it lacked a health exception. We noted that there existed a "division of medical opinion" about the relative safety of intact D&E, ... but we made clear that as long as "substantial medical authority supports the proposition that banning a particular abortion procedure could endanger women's health," a health exception is required. We explained:

> "The word 'necessary' in *Casey*'s phrase 'necessary, in appropriate medical judgment, for the preservation of the life or health of the [pregnant woman],' cannot refer to an absolute necessity or to absolute proof. Medical treatments and procedures are often considered appropriate (or inappropriate) in light of estimated comparative health risks (and health benefits) in particular cases. Neither can that phrase require unanimity of medical opinion. Doctors often differ in their estimation of comparative health risks and appropriate treatment. And *Casey*'s words 'appropriate medical judgment' must embody the judicial need to tolerate responsible differences of medical opinion...."

Thus, we reasoned, division in medical opinion "at most means uncertainty, a factor that signals the presence of risk, not its absence." ...

Ban Contains Many Inaccuracies

In 2003, a few years after our ruling in *Stenberg*, Congress passed the Partial-Birth Abortion Ban Act—without an exception for women's health. The congressional findings on which the Partial-Birth Abortion Ban Act rests do not withstand inspection, as the lower courts have determined and this Court is obliged to concede.

Many of the Act's recitations are incorrect. For example, Congress determined that no medical schools provide instruction on intact D&E. But in fact, numerous leading medical schools teach the procedure.

More important, Congress claimed there was a medical consensus that the banned procedure is never necessary. But the evidence "very clearly demonstrate[d] the opposite."

Similarly, Congress found that "[t]here is no credible medical evidence that partial-birth abortions are safe or are safer than other abortion procedures." But the congressional record includes letters from numerous individual physicians stating that pregnant women's health would be jeopardized under the Act, as well as statements from nine professional associations, including ACOG, the American Public Health Association, and the California Medical Association, attesting that intact D&E carries meaningful safety advantages over other methods. No comparable medical groups supported the ban. In fact, "all of the government's own witnesses disagreed with many of the specific congressional findings."

District Court's Findings

In contrast to Congress, the District Courts made findings after full trials at which all parties had the opportunity to present their best evidence. The courts had the benefit of "much more extensive medical and scientific evidence . . . concerning the safety and necessity of intact D&Es."

During the District Court trials, "numerous" "extraordinarily accomplished" and "very experienced" medical experts explained that, in certain circumstances and for certain women, intact D&E is safer than alternative procedures and necessary to protect women's health.

According to the expert testimony plaintiffs introduced, the safety advantages of intact D&E are marked for women with certain medical conditions, for example, uterine scarring, bleeding disorders, heart disease, or compromised immune systems. Further plaintiffs' experts testified that intact D&E is significantly safer for women with certain pregnancy-related conditions, such as placenta previa and accreta, and for women carrying fetuses with certain abnormalities, such as severe hydrocephalus.

Intact D&E, plaintiffs' experts explained, provides safety benefits over D&E by dismemberment for several reasons: *First,* intact D&E minimizes the number of times a physician must insert instruments through the cervix and into the uterus, and thereby reduces the risk of trauma to, and perforation of, the cervix and uterus—the most serious complication associated with nonintact D&E. *Second,* removing the fetus intact, instead of dismembering it *in utero,* decreases the likelihood that fetal tissue will be retained in the uterus, a condition that can cause infection, hemorrhage, and infertility. *Third,* intact D&E diminishes the chances of exposing the patient's tissues to sharp bony fragments sometimes resulting from dismemberment of the fetus. *Fourth,* intact D&E takes less operating time than D&E by dismemberment, and thus may reduce bleeding, the risk of infection, and complications relating to anesthesia.

Support for Necessity of D&E

Based on thoroughgoing review of the trial evidence and the congressional record, each of the District Courts to consider the issue rejected Congress' findings as unreasonable and not supported by the evidence. The trial courts concluded, in contrast to Congress' findings, that "significant medical authority supports the proposition that in some circumstances, [intact D&E] is the safest procedure."

The District Courts' findings merit this Court's respect. Today's opinion supplies no reason to reject those findings. Nevertheless, despite the District Courts' appraisal of the weight of the evidence, and in undisguised conflict with *Stenberg,* the Court asserts that the Partial-Birth Abortion Ban Act can survive "when . . . medical uncertainty persists." This assertion is bewildering. Not only does it defy the Court's long-standing precedent affirming the necessity of a health exception, with no carve-out for circumstances of medical uncertainty; it gives short shrift to the records before us, carefully canvassed by the District Courts. Those records indicate that "the majority of highly-qualified experts on the subject believe intact D&E to be the safest, most appropriate procedure under certain circumstances."

The Court acknowledges some of this evidence, but insists that, because some witnesses disagreed with the ACOG and other experts' assessment of risk, the Act can stand. In this insistence, the Court brushes under the rug the District Courts' well-supported findings that the physicians who testified that intact D&E is never necessary to preserve the health of a woman had slim authority for their opinions. They had no training for, or personal experience with, the intact D&E procedure, and many performed abortions only on rare occasions. Even indulging the assumption that the Government witnesses were equally qualified to evaluate the relative risks of abortion procedures, their testimony could not erase the "significant medical authority support[ing] the proposition that in some circumstances, [intact D&E] would be the safest procedure."

Applying to Other Abortion Procedures

The Court offers flimsy and transparent justifications for upholding a nationwide ban on intact D&E *sans* any exception to safeguard a women's health. Today's ruling, the Court declares, advances "a premise central to [*Casey*'s] conclusion"— *i.e.*, the Government's "legitimate and substantial interest in preserving and promoting fetal life." But the Act scarcely furthers that interest: The law saves not a single fetus from destruction, for it targets only a *method* of performing abortion. And surely the statute was not designed to protect the lives or health of pregnant women. In short, the Court upholds a law that, while doing nothing to "preserv[e] ... fetal life," bars a woman from choosing intact D&E although her doctor "reasonably believes [that procedure] will best protect [her]."

As another reason for upholding the ban, the Court emphasizes that the Act does not proscribe the nonintact D&E procedure. But why not, one might ask. Nonintact D&E could equally be characterized as "brutal," involving as it does "tear-[ing] [a fetus] apart" and "ripp[ing] off" its limbs.

Delivery of an intact, albeit nonviable, fetus warrants special condemnation, the Court maintains, because a fetus that is not dismembered resembles an infant. But so, too, does a fetus delivered intact after it is terminated by injection a day or two before the surgical evacuation, or a fetus delivered through medical induction or cesarean. Yet, the availability of those procedures—along with D&E by dismemberment—the Court says, saves the ban on intact D&E from a declaration of unconstitutionality. Never mind that the procedures deemed acceptable might put a woman's health at greater risk.

A Step Backward for Women

Ultimately, the Court admits that "moral concerns" are at work, concerns that could yield prohibitions on any abortion. Notably, the concerns expressed are untethered to any ground genuinely serving the Government's interest in preserving life. By allowing such concerns to carry the day and case, overriding fundamental rights, the Court dishonors our precedent.

Revealing in this regard, the Court invokes an antiabortion shibboleth for which it concededly has no reliable evidence: Women who have abortions come to regret their choices, and consequently suffer from "[s]evere depression and loss of esteem." Because of women's fragile emotional state and because of the "bond of love the mother has for her child," the Court worries, doctors may withhold information about the nature of the intact D&E procedure. The solution the Court approves, then, is *not* to require doctors to inform women, accurately and adequately, of the different procedures and their attendant risks. Instead, the Court deprives women of the right to make an autonomous choice, even at the expense of their safety.

This way of thinking reflects ancient notions about women's place in the family and under the Constitution—ideas that have long since been discredited.

> "Congress's finding that intact D&Es are 'never medically indicated to preserve the health of the mother' ... [was] discredited by overwhelming evidence presented at three separate federal court trials."

The Importance of Dilation and Extraction to Women's Health

Stephen Chasen et al.

The following viewpoint is an excerpt from the amicus curiae (friend of the court) brief on behalf of physician LeRoy Carhart and the Planned Parenthood Federation of America in the case of Gonzales v. Carhart *(2007), in which the Supreme Court upheld the Partial-Birth Abortion Ban Act of 2003. Chasen and six other practicing experts in the field of obstetrics and gynecology emphatically disagree with Congress's findings that intact D&E (intact dilation and evacuation, also known as D&X or dilation and extraction, the medical procedure called "partial-birth abortion" by opponents of abortion) "is never medically necessary and should be prohibited." They argue that D&Es of all variations have safety advantages over other methods and that the safety advantages are especially important for women who are at risk for catastrophic complications.*

Amici, plaintiffs in *NAF v. Gonzales* ("Plaintiffs"), challenged the Act because it is constitutionally deficient on numerous grounds, including that it bans an array of safe

Stephen Chasen et al., amicus brief, *Gonzales v. Carhart*, U.S. Supreme Court, (Carhart II), 2007.

abortion procedures. But even if the Act prohibited only second-trimester surgical abortions in which the fetus is removed intact—as the government sometimes claims—it would still unconstitutionally endanger women's health. *Amici* refer to these procedures as intact dilation and evacuation ("intact D&E"), because they are among the variants of dilation and evacuation ("D&E"), which collectively account for the vast majority of second-trimester abortions.

Essentially ignoring the Act's other flaws, the government's defense of the Act relies almost entirely on Congress's finding that intact D&Es are "never medically indicated to preserve the health of the mother." This claim—and Congress's findings—were discredited by overwhelming evidence presented at three separate federal-court trials held simultaneously in the Spring of 2004. At those trials, eminent experts from the faculties of leading medical schools, who have years of experience both performing abortions and treating women facing high-risk pregnancies, testified that D&E with intact removal offers significant safety advantages over alternative methods of terminating a pregnancy in the second trimester. These witnesses testified to the considerable health benefits of removing the fetus as intact as possible, and to the particular benefit of doing so for women in compromised medical states. After hearing this evidence, all three district courts concluded that banning such procedures without a health exception violates the Constitution and this Court's clear commands.

The New York district court, like the Nebraska and California courts whose decisions are under review, concluded that Congress's legislative findings cannot withstand even the most deferential review. The New York court found that there is "no consensus that D&X is never medically necessary," and that, in fact, "there is a significant body of medical opinion that holds the contrary." The New York court's conclusions were based on a substantial record amassed from over twenty witnesses, from twelve of the most acclaimed medical and academic institutions in the country, during a three-week trial. The record in New York comports fully with those under review in this case and in *Planned Parenthood Federation of America v. Ashcroft* (2004). That the New York court did not credit certain of Plaintiffs' evidence does not undermine that court's central and dispositive finding: that there is substantial medical authority supporting the proposition that prohibiting intact D&E endangers women's health. This finding adds considerable further weight to support affirmance.

Expert Witnesses in New York Case

In November 2003, roughly simultaneously with the filing of the two cases currently under review by this Court, Plaintiffs brought suit in the United States District Court for the Southern District of New York challenging the Act. On November 6, 2003, the New York court issued a temporary restraining order (TRO) and, with the consent of the government, later extended the TRO pending final resolution of the case. During a three-week trial in March and April 2004, the court heard testimony from sixteen witnesses in person and six by deposition. On August 26, 2004, the court issued a decision permanently enjoining the Act as unconstitutional under this Court's precedents because it lacks a health exception. On January 31, 2006, the Second Circuit affirmed, holding that "the lack of a health exception renders the Act unconstitutional." The Second Circuit deferred ruling on the appropriate remedy until supplemental briefs could be filed addressing this Court's recent ruling in *Ayotte v. Planned Parenthood* (2006). That briefing was thereafter stayed pending the outcome of this case.

The New York court recognized seven of Plaintiffs' witnesses (including the five Plaintiffs who testified at trial) as experts in obstetrics and gynecology and abortion practice and procedures. These experts are all professors in the obstetrics and gynecology departments at leading medical schools. Dr. Timothy Johnson is department chair at the University of

Michigan; Dr. Gerson Weiss is department chair at UMDNJ-New Jersey Medical School; Drs. Amos Grunebaum and Stephen Chasen teach at Cornell University; Drs. Cassing Hammond and Marilynn Frederiksen teach at Northwestern University; and Dr. Carolyn Westhoff teaches at Columbia University. Collectively, they have extensive experience both performing and teaching the abortion methods at issue in this case. They have all performed first- and second-trimester abortions, and have used both of the procedures commonly used to terminate pregnancies in the second trimester, D&E and induction. Each of these experts has either performed, or personally observed, the variant of D&E involving intact removal of the fetus. These experts teach an array of obstetric and gynecological procedures, including abortion; most of them teach D&E with intact removal.

Five experts testified at trial for the government. Each of the government's experts had limited, if any, experience with abortion practice. Not one of the government's experts had any experience with D&E involving intact removal. None had even personally observed such a procedure.

Expert Testimony on Abortion Methods

As the undisputed testimony showed and the New York district court found, approximately 90% of all abortions occur during the first trimester of pregnancy, and approximately 10% during the second. During the second trimester (which begins at thirteen to fourteen weeks from the first day of the woman's last menstrual period before she became pregnant ("LMP")), approximately 95% of abortions are performed using the D&E method.

D&E consists of dilating the cervix and evacuating the uterus. Both Plaintiffs' and the government's witnesses testified that the physician's goal in any D&E is to empty the uterus in the safest way possible for the woman.

In a D&E, the physician first dilates and softens the cervix so that the uterus can be safely evacuated. To achieve adequate dilation, physicians typically place osmotic dilators in the cervix, which expand slowly as they absorb moisture from the cervix, thereby gradually opening it. Once dilation is adequate, the physician inserts instruments or his or her fingers through the dilated cervix and into the uterus, to grasp the fetus. The physician then uses traction (*i.e.*, pulling) to remove the fetus from the uterus.

Definition of a D&E Procedure

As the New York record demonstrates, during a D&E, the fetus may be removed intact or in parts. Both parties' experts testified that physicians performing D&Es seek to minimize the number of times they insert instruments into the uterus. They therefore try to remove as much of the fetus as possible with each pass of an instrument. In some cases, depending on factors such as the degree of cervical dilation achieved, the tensile strength of the fetal tissue, and the position of the fetus, the physician is able to remove the fetus intact or relatively intact with the first pass of instruments. The experts in New York testified, however, that despite attempts to remove the fetus as intact as possible, the process often results in removal of the fetus in parts, with the physician reinserting instruments—and extracting as much of the fetus as possible with each instrument pass—until the evacuation is complete.

A variety of terms—such as "intact D&E" or "D&X"— were used throughout the New York trial to describe second-trimester surgical abortions in which the fetus is removed intact or largely intact. Regardless of the term employed, the New York experts testified that such a procedure is "a variation of . . . D&E."

Any D&E Procedure Banned

The testimony in New York showed that virtually all of the remaining second-trimester procedures (five percent) are performed using the induction method. In an induction abortion, which can last anywhere from fewer than twelve hours to more than forty-eight hours, pre-term labor is initiated with medication, the cervix dilates, and the fetus is generally expelled through the labor process. In some induction abortions, however, the physician must intervene with surgical steps to complete the evacuation as safely as possible for the woman. When this happens, the physician uses the surgical techniques of D&E to complete the procedure.

The uncontested evidence presented in the New York trial established that any D&E or induction—whether used to induce abortion or to treat pregnancy loss (sometimes called "miscarriage")—may fall within the definition of "partial-birth abortion" contained in the Act.

The remaining procedures for pregnancy termination in the second trimester, hysterectomy (removal of the uterus) and hysterotomy (essentially a pre-term cesarean section), are rarely used to terminate pregnancies because of their inherent risks and consequences for future reproduction. They nonetheless remain legal and can be used in those unusual circumstances in which they may be the safest method for a given patient with a critical medical condition.

Importance of Intact D&E

The extensive evidence presented in New York is entirely consistent with that presented in the Nebraska and California cases under review. The New York court heard "more evidence during its trial than Congress heard over the span of eight years," including testimony from a greater number of physicians on the safety of D&E involving intact removal. In addition to Plaintiffs' highly credentialed experts, who testified to the significant safety advantages of intact D&E, several of the government's experts acknowledged that such procedures may reduce the risk of dire complications and provide safety advantages for some patients. That evidence demonstrated that intact D&E is well within the standard of care; that it is becoming ever more widely used as greater numbers of physicians learn this approach to D&E and read about its benefits in the medical literature; and that a ban on its use would harm women's health.

Accordingly, like the courts whose decisions are under review, the New York trial court found that "[t]here is no consensus that D&X is never medically necessary, but there is a significant body of medical opinion that holds the contrary." This conclusion, affirmed by the Second Circuit, places the New York decision in an unbroken line that has struck down laws banning intact D&E since this Court's decision in *Stenberg v. Carhart* (2000).

Like the courts in Nebraska and California, the New York court concluded that Congress's findings were belied by both the congressional record itself and abundant trial evidence. Having observed that "[e]ven the government's own experts disagreed with almost all of Congress's factual findings," the court held that those findings cannot satisfy even the highly deferential standard the government urged. The court, that is, found that the findings do not even reflect "reasonable inferences based on substantial evidence."

No Medical Consensus

The New York court rejected Congress's finding that there is a "consensus" that D&E with intact removal "is never medically necessary and should be prohibited." . . .

In addition to the congressional record, the New York court found that the "[t]estimony adduced at trial bolsters this conclusion" that Congress was "unreasonable to conclude that a consensus within the medical community" opposes intact D&E. That testimony includes the concessions of the government's own witnesses that no such consensus exists.

Abundant trial evidence likewise disproved Congress's other "findings." For example, Congress asserted that intact

D&E was not taught at any medical schools. Yet, "[t]estimony at trial adduced that, contrary to Congress's finding, the procedure is taught at leading medical schools," including, as experts for both sides testified, Columbia, Cornell, New York University, Northwestern, and Albert Einstein College of Medicine. Dr. Lockwood, a witness for the government and Chair of the obstetrics and gynecology department at Yale Medical School, testified that intact D&E was taught under his chairmanship at New York University, and that he "intends to develop a program at Yale which would teach the procedure." Currently, at least six additional medical schools, including Yale, provide instruction on this surgical technique. The record likewise reflects that authoritative medical textbooks discuss intact D&E and its safety benefits.

The Safety Advantages

The New York trial record supports the safety advantages of intact D&E based on three demonstrated facts: (1) D&Es of all variations have safety advantages over induction abortions, (2) D&Es with intact removal have safety advantages over D&Es with dismemberment, and (3) these safety advantages are especially important for women who are particularly vulnerable to catastrophic complications by virtue of their already compromised medical states.

First, it is uncontested that prohibiting D&Es in general would endanger women's health. At the New York trial, all parties' experts agreed that, while D&E and induction are both extremely safe procedures, D&E is generally safer than induction at certain stages of pregnancy. It was also undisputed that for numerous women, induction is dramatically less safe than D&E. These patients include, for example, women at high risk of uterine rupture during an induction, due to prior scarring from procedures such as high (also known as "classical") cesarean sections or from the surgical removal of uterine fibroids.

Second, the evidence presented in New York showed that numerous physicians believe that, among D&E variants, D&E involving intact removal may be the *safest* way—although not the only way—to terminate a pregnancy in the second trimester. Even the government's experts agreed that there are intuitive advantages to intact removal. Indeed, government witness Dr. Lockwood conceded that, compared to dismembering the fetus, intact removal might carry lower risks of injury to the woman. . . .

Third, the New York record also included abundant evidence that intact removal may be the safest option for women with certain medical conditions who are terminating their pregnancies. In such cases, the benefits described above are particularly important given the patient's already compromised medical state and increased vulnerability to catastrophic complications. These conditions include, for example, being prone to or having infection, experiencing, or being at risk for, chorioamnionitis, a potentially deadly infection of the amniotic fluid and membranes that, among other things, increases the risk of uterine perforation, being otherwise at risk of hemorrhage, having compromised immune systems; and being prone to perforation or having uterine scarring. In addition, ACOG's [the American College of Obstetricians and Gynecologists] expert panel pointed to numerous such conditions that make intact D&E the safest abortion method for certain patients. In addition to these conditions, there was also testimony in New York that D&E with intact removal could benefit women carrying fetuses with certain anomalies, such as hydrocephaly (which greatly enlarges the fetal head), and that it may also help in the post-abortion pathological diagnosis of certain fetal conditions.

In sum, there was ample evidence in New York from highly credentialed experts on both sides to support the conclusion that banning intact D&E without a health exception creates "unnecessary risk of tragic health consequences." The evidence showed that the unique advantages of intact removal—reduction of instrument passes, fetal fragmentation, procedure time—minimize the likelihood of complications that, while perhaps infrequent in an absolute sense, are potentially catastrophic in the very real cases when they do occur. The potential consequences of these complications include hemorrhage, overwhelming and systemic infection, and infertility. Such potentially catastrophic complications are no less constitutionally cognizable simply because they are, fortunately, rare.

> "Pro-life Americans must work . . . with the same sense of determination and strategic genius [to reverse Roe v. Wade] that the NAACP . . . used in eroding the precedent of Plessy v. Ferguson."

Gonzales v. Carhart Suggests a Strategy for Overturning *Roe v. Wade*

Steven G. Calabresi

Steven G. Calabresi cofounded the Federalist Society, serves as chairman of the society's board of directors, and is a professor of constitutional law at Northwestern University School of Law.

In the viewpoint below, Calabresi argues that Roe v. Wade (1973), which granted women a constitutional right to an abortion, is an "immoral" law like Plessy v. Ferguson (1896), which instituted "separate but equal" legislation for black and white Americans. He likens the pro-life movement to the early civil rights movement and recommends that pro-life activists follow the model set by civil rights leaders in the 1950s by challenging Roe in court and by changing public opinion. He contends that the Court's ruling in Gonzales v. Carhart (2007), which upheld the Partial-Birth Abortion Ban Act of 2003, takes an important step toward eroding Roe.

Steven G. Calabresi, "How to Reverse Government Imposition of Immorality: A Strategy for Eroding *Roe v. Wade*," *Harvard Journal of Law & Public Policy*, vol. 31, 2008, pp. 85–92. Copyright © 2006 by the President and Fellows of Harvard College. Reproduced by permission.

There is . . . one important respect in which our law is deeply immoral: its recognition of *a constitutional right* of women to have abortions. In the United States, we have not merely decriminalized or legalized abortion. We have made the legality of abortion a matter of individual constitutional right. In so doing, the American legal system has put its highest moral imprimatur on a loathsome procedure that ought to be at least discouraged by the law if not forbidden altogether. *Roe v. Wade* was thus in my opinion not merely wrongly decided. It was also profoundly immoral.

This Essay lays out a plan for righting that wrong. It describes how pro-life groups can erode the precedential value of *Roe*, paving the way for its overruling, and legally discourage abortion once again. In the process, this essay makes two suggestions which should be useful to those who wish to reverse other legal trends they find unfortunate—for example, the extensive constitutional protection our legal system gives to pornography or our unusual use of the death penalty as a form of punishment.

First, those working against *Roe* must understand that public opinion matters. Just as there are limits on the government's ability to legislate morality (as the experiment of Prohibition taught us) without at least some degree of public support, so too is it the case that the Supreme Court will not overrule incorrect or immoral decisions when the public clearly opposes its doing so. For better or worse, each part of the struggle against abortion—the legislative *and* the constitutional—requires building up public support.

Second, Americans who oppose abortion must candidly discuss strategy. We must learn to litigate shrewdly and to shape public opinion. On both scores, we would be well-advised to adopt some of the legal tactics employed in past moral constitutional campaigns—for example the campaigns against capital punishment and racial segregation. To prevail, supporters of the pro-life cause must adapt old means used in these prior campaigns to the new end of cutting back on *Roe.* . . .

Strategy of Civil Rights Activists

Pro-life Americans must work to erode the precedents of *Roe v. Wade* and *Planned Parenthood of Southeastern Pennsylvania v. Casey* with the same sense of determination and strategic genius that the NAACP [National Association for the Advancement of Colored People] Legal Defense Fund used in eroding the precedent of *Plessy v. Ferguson.* It is worth noting in this regard that the NAACP's campaign against *Plessy* was a protracted one, beginning in the 1930s, achieving a major victory twenty years later in *Brown v. Board of Education,* and only realizing complete success with the 1967 decision *Loving v. Virginia,* more than thirty years after the campaign against Jim Crow [segregation] had begun. This final victory in *Loving*—which declared anti-miscegenation laws to be unconstitutional—came only after Congress had weighed in on the pro-civil rights side with the Civil Rights Act of 1964 and the Voting Rights Act of 1965. I do not think Americans necessarily need to wait twenty or thirty years to overrule *Roe.* Indeed, we may well be closer to being able to attain that objective than we realize, even if we are much further away from having a political climate in which even the most extreme forms of abortion can again be made illegal. . . .

I suspect that Justice [Anthony] Kennedy may understand the *Casey* plurality opinion to mean that most regulations of abortion commanding fifty percent support in national public opinion polls are constitutional. In the capital punishment area, Justice Kennedy has not hesitated to give constitutional weight to modern public opinion opposing the execution of the mentally infirm or of juveniles, and he might give similar weight to public opinion with respect to regulations of abortion. It is worth noting in this regard that the plurality opinion in *Casey* upheld the imposition of waiting periods and parental consent for abortions for minors, both of which were supported by majorities in national public opinion polls. *Casey* did strike down the Pennsylvania spousal notification requirement, which commanded more than fifty percent support in national public opinion polls. But it is possible that Justice Kennedy agreed to this largely as a sop to Justices [Sandra Day] O'Connor and [David] Souter, allowing the three of them to collaborate together on the *Casey* plurality opinion. Regardless of his reason for acting the way he did at that time, I personally do not expect Justice Kennedy ever again to overturn a regulation of abortion with majority support in national opinion polls.

The key to eroding *Roe v. Wade*, then, is to pass a number of state or federal laws that restrict abortion rights in ways approved of by at least fifty percent of the public in national public opinion polls. Those cases can then be litigated up to the Supreme Court, and we can begin to build up a body of pro-life case law, like *Gonzales v. Carhart*. Once we have won enough such cases, the Court will be in a position to overrule *Roe*. I think there may well be a substantial period of time where *Roe* is not technically "overruled" but during which it will be rendered meaningless. This is what happened to *Lochner v. New York* which became a dead letter in 1937, but which was not formally overturned until the Court's decision in *Ferguson v. Skrupa* in 1963. [*Lochner* and *Ferguson* were two Supreme court cases dealing with the Due Process Clause of the Fourteenth Amendment.] Despite any temporary delay in its formal overruling, however, the days of *Roe* would be numbered.

Employing a Gradualist Strategy

I am not an expert on national public opinion polling on abortion, so I will defer to others to develop the precise content of the kind of abortion restrictions that might pass muster with Justice Kennedy. Offhand, I would recommend passing laws like the following: a ban on abortion for sex selection, a law preventing boyfriends or parents from intimidating young women into choosing to have an abortion, a ban on any form of abortion that might cause pain to the fetus (such as by sucking out his or her brain, or hacking his or her body into pieces), and a nationally-applicable mandatory waiting period before abortions can be performed. The pro-life movement should borrow a page here from the opponents of capital punishment, who challenge every mode of execution, from hanging to lethal injection, as imposing cruel and unusual punishment. Opponents of abortion should raise the same kinds of challenges, one by one, to each abortion procedure. This will force the public to focus on exactly what abortion entails, and that will put us on the national majority side of the issue. The end goal should be to have all abortion procedures banned nationally.

My strategy for eroding *Roe* thus advocates gradualism rather than immediate and outright challenges. If the recent South Dakota law banning abortion, for example, had survived its brush with the voters, Justice Kennedy might have struck it down because national public opinion polls reveal a majority opposed to "overruling" *Roe*. I thus think that the pro-life cause is best advanced by slowly tightening the regulatory noose around abortion, and would suffer a setback were *Roe* challenged head on.

In order to overrule *Roe*, therefore, we must arrive at a situation where a majority of the public supports overruling *Roe*. We will need such a majority not only to get Justice Kennedy's vote, but also to confirm new originalist Justices, to pass new laws restricting abortion, and to make sure that prosecutors enforce those new laws. Here, I think opponents of abortion need a massive public education campaign that informs citizens about the facts of fetal development and that puts the moral authority of government on the side of discouraging resort to abortion.

We do not have too far to go. Former President Bill and [former] Senator Hillary Rodham Clinton, for example, still claim they want abortion to be safe, legal, *and rare*. The Clintons need to be called on their rhetoric. If they truly mean it when they say that they want abortion to be rare, they should have no objection to starting a massive, federally-funded educational campaign to discourage abortion and encourage adoption. This campaign could and should be modeled on the federal government's highly successful campaign over the last forty years to end smoking. . . .

I predict that by following this course we would, eventually, change public opinion to the point where even Justice Kennedy will be prepared to overrule *Roe* if he is still on the Supreme Court. But more importantly, such a public campaign to advertise the immorality of abortion will create a climate in which pro-life Supreme Court nominees, laws, and decisions to prosecute abortionists will flourish. Since our goal is not merely to erode *Roe* but actually to protect unborn life, we need to bring Congress and public opinion over to our side of this issue. Overruling *Roe* without creating a climate in which at least some abortionists can be and are in fact prosecuted would be a meaningless victory.

"Abortion-rights advocates can frame abortion as a matter of social justice, not just of freedom from government interference."

The Pro-choice Movement Should Adopt a Social Justice Platform

Rebecca Tuhus-Dubrow

Brooklyn-based journalist Rebecca Tuhus-Dubrow is a contributing writer for the Boston Globe's *Ideas section, the* Nation, *Salon,* Believer, *and* Dissent *magazines.*

In the following viewpoint, Tuhus-Dubrow argues that mainstream feminism's use of "choice" rhetoric has been co-opted by a consumer culture that offers superficial choices, thus undermining the importance of reproductive control. She urges supporters of abortion rights to embrace an emphasis on reproductive justice, which includes social justice issues important to communities of color and working-class women.

The link between reproductive rights and eugenics is not new; in fact, it has dogged the [pro-choice] movement since its early days. Margaret Sanger, the tireless pioneer of birth control in the United States, started out in the early twentieth century as a radical socialist and feminist. A nurse with working-class origins, she saw firsthand the travails of poor women drained physically and financially by endless births. Sanger believed that birth control—legally restricted at

Rebecca Tuhus-Dubrow, "Designer Babies and the Pro-choice Movement," *Dissent*, vol. 54, Summer 2007, pp. 37–43. Copyright © 2007 by Dissent Publishing Corporation. Reproduced by permission.

the time—was all but a panacea for society's ills. She launched a crusade, even subordinating other values to the cause: during World War I, for example, she kept quiet about her pacifist beliefs out of fear that her unpopular opinion would undermine support for birth control.

By 1919, Sanger's far-left political background was a liability in a climate hostile to radicalism. At the same time, the eugenics movement was seen as socially responsible and forward-thinking by the public and many intellectuals. Eugenicists argued that society would benefit if families with "good genes" reproduced prolifically, while the "unfit" refrained from procreating. . . .

Targeting the Poor

In an attempt to gain the imprimatur of science, and in a move that has since haunted her legacy, Sanger became associated with the eugenics movement. She had promoted birth control for the poor because she saw that they suffered most for the lack of it. The well-off always managed to procure means for controlling their fertility; Sanger's poor patients begged her for the secrets of the rich. When she embraced eugenics, her rhetoric adapted easily to the values of the movement. "While I personally believe in the sterilization of the feeble-minded, the insane and the syphiletic [sic]," she wrote in 1919, "I have not been able to discover that these measures are more than superficial deterrents when applied to the constantly growing stream of the unfit. . . . Birth control, on the other hand, not only opens the way to the eugenist [sic], but it preserves his work."

This early association, along with certain government policies, helped to taint birth control and abortion in the eyes of many minorities. Plenty of poor white people suffered under eugenic policies, but black, Hispanic, and indigenous women were targeted disproportionately. (In the rural South, sterilizations of black women—often performed without their knowledge following childbirth, abortion, or other operations—were known as the "Mississippi appendectomy," a term coined by [civil rights activist] Fannie Lou Hamer to describe her own.) In the 1960s and 1970s, the Black Panther Party and the Nation of Islam both denounced birth control as genocidal. Other groups, such as the National Association for the Advancement of Colored People and the Student Non-violent Coordinating Committee, also harbored suspicions. When the government funded birth control rather than health care or child care in poor communities, some activists angrily pointed out that reducing the number of poor people was not the same as reducing poverty. Fears ran deep that contraception and abortion, as well as sterilization, were means of controlling, if not eliminating, these communities.

Feminists Adopt Rhetoric of Choice

Meanwhile, the mainstream pro-choice movement was operating from a vastly different perspective. Mainstream feminists wanted the choice *not* to have children, to be emancipated from the constraints of the traditional female role. Rarely, did white women have to fight to have children; the struggle was to avoid having them. In the 1960s and 1970s, abortion rights activists framed the debate in terms of feminism and sexual liberation. The movement triumphed with *Roe v. Wade* [(1973); the Supreme Court ruling legalizing abortion].

In the following decades, some strands of the mainstream pro-choice movement, notably NARAL (then known as the National Abortion Rights Action League), modified their approach in the face of changing political realities. In the aftermath of the *Webster v. Reproductive Health Services* Supreme Court decision (1989), which upheld a Missouri statute prohibiting the use of public facilities for abortions, NARAL launched its successful "Who Decides?" campaign, which toned down the women's liberation language and focused on the right to freedom from government intervention. As Kate Michelman, until recently NARAL's president, recalls in her 2005 book, *With Liberty and Justice for All,* "The issue was not whether abortion was morally right or wrong; that was a matter of individual conscience. The question was, who had the right to decide—women or the government?" On the defensive against a passionately committed (and sometimes murderous) anti-abortion movement, many feminists focused more intensively on abortion, shifting energy away from other goals, such as child care, maternity leave, and support for alternative sexual lifestyles. All of these had once been integral parts of the feminist pro-choice agenda. . . .

Although arguably a political necessity at the time, focusing on abortion and adopting an individual liberties paradigm had its costs. . . . One was the loss of a compelling moral narrative, which left a vacuum for the anti-abortion side to fill. Another was the alienation of poor minority women. Abortion was less of a priority for women struggling with multiple reproductive challenges: environmental hazards, lack of health care and child care, the fear of coerced sterilization. Some of those who wanted abortions couldn't afford to pay for them, so the freedom from government intervention was inadequate. The racial component of reproductive politics has been analyzed by scholars such as Dorothy Roberts in *Killing the Black Body* and Jennifer Nelson in *Women of Color and the Reproductive Rights Movement.*

Choice Rhetoric and Consumerism

Currently, the pro-choice movement is under siege to a greater degree than any time since 1973, a situation that has led it to reassess its strategy. Now, some supporters of abortion rights want to move beyond the stagnant terms of the debate. Efforts to rethink the conventional approach are evident in the work of Frances Kissling, former president of Catholics for a Free Choice; "reproductive justice" advocates, including Loretta Ross; mainstream players in the Democratic Party, such as George Lakoff, a linguist and consultant; and would-be [2008] presidential nominee Hillary Clinton; as well as many other feminists and activists. The term "choice" itself has come under scrutiny, often criticized as a problematic concept and a weak and morally flaccid competitor with "life." Recent documents, such as *Beyond Choice*, a 2004 book by Alexander Sanger, grandson of Margaret and chair of the International Planned Parenthood Council, and *More than a Choice*, a 2006 paper by the Center for American Progress, reflect this attitude.

Choice rhetoric has seeped into other aspects of feminism as well, with mixed results. Linda Hirschman caused a stir in 2005 with an article in the *American Prospect* decrying "choice feminism"—the notion that staying home with the kids is as feminist as working, provided that it's the woman's "choice." Her article focused on the "mommy wars" debate, but the same rationale can apply to other aspects of female life. Some women assert that anything from wearing lipstick to topless dancing can be a feminist act, because a woman is empowered by her choice to perform it. . . . Hirschman argued that women, with the goal of collective advancement in mind, ought to aggressively pursue high-power, high-paying positions.

Although I don't agree with everything Hirschman wrote—for instance, that we should eschew low-paying, socially beneficial work in favor of cutthroat corporate success—I think she was onto something. "Choice feminism" is uncomfortably close to the ethos of consumer culture. A feminism that consecrates individual choices, endorsing them all as equally valid, has lost its mission and its soul. (Indeed, "choice feminism" is Hirschman's term, not a movement with an agenda; but some women do subscribe to the idea.)

Reproductive Technologies and Designer Babies

And here is where the reprogenetic technologies fit in. What is a "designer baby" but a new consumer choice? When a vague, distorted feminism is conflated with enthusiastic consumerism, when "choice" is the catchword of both, designer babies can easily emerge as the natural, if not inevitable, next step in the evolution of our liberated, capitalist society, in which choices will continue to multiply for consumers—especially for those consumers par excellence, women. . . .

The first and least controversial task for pro-choice activists, then, is to make it very clear that the rights for which they have fought are fundamentally different from the right to determine the genetic makeup of offspring. Whether the latter right is legitimate or not, it is not the same as or an extension of the former. Pro-choice activists have struggled for women's freedom to control their own lives and bodies, not to control the lives and bodies of their children.

Drawing this distinction could lead to another step: emphasizing the morality of abortion rights. Abortion should be legal because women should have the same rights as men to shape their lives; because sometimes bringing a child into the world is the wrong thing to do; because without legal abortion, women suffer and die. Abortion-rights advocates can frame abortion as a matter of social justice, not just of freedom from government interference.

The Importance of Reproductive Justice

As an alternative to "choice," women of color have created the concept of "reproductive justice." In the literature of Sister-Song Women of Color Reproductive Health Collective, the national coordinator, Loretta Ross, defines the term, coined in 1994, as "(1) the right to have a child; (2) the right not to have a child; (3) the right to parent the children we have. . . . We also fight for the necessary enabling conditions to realize these rights." This more comprehensive notion of reproductive justice can be useful in confronting the issue of designer babies. Although not currently one of the main items on the reproductive justice agenda, a position on reprogenetic technologies can easily be added to the list of concerns, which include environmental hazards and health care. In fact, of the reproductive rights activists I've spoken to, Ross was the most sympathetic to the prospect of regulating these technologies.

As [Carole] Joffe pointed out in the *Dissent* article ["It's Not *Just* Abortion, Stupid," Winter 2005], "the logic of seeing abortion as just one part of the mosaic of reproductive and sexual rights and services is not simply that it is persuasive to others. It is also the most authentic position of the reproductive freedom movement itself." Reproductive technologies did not factor into the original movement, because they didn't yet exist. But now that they do, promoting sensible policies on their use should fit into a broader platform. Such a platform could appeal to other factions of the left as well as moderates, who might be turned off by the focus on abortion but who share concerns about related issues, including the abuse of reprogenetic technologies.

The concept of reproductive justice has already made inroads into the mainstream movement. The pro-choice movement eludes generalization, because different organizations have different priorities and approaches, but many parts of it have already begun to shift toward a social justice focus and a broader platform. The literature of Choice USA, a fifteen-year-old organization founded by [feminist leader] Gloria Steinem, uses the term reproductive justice, and Planned Parenthood sponsored a conference in 2005 at Smith College titled "Reproductive Justice for All."

Concerns About Reprogenetics

Concerns about reprogenetics have also surfaced. The Planned Parenthood conference devoted a quarter of the agenda to reproductive technologies. The Center for Genetics and Society, billed as "a pro-choice organization working for sensible policies on genetic engineering technology," aims to initiate and facilitate conversations about the subject. One effort was a retreat in October 2006 with representatives from various progressive organizations, including Planned Parenthood, Choice USA, the ACLU [American Civil Liberties Union], the disability rights group Not Dead Yet, and the LGBT [lesbian, gay, bisexual, and transgendered] Community Center of New York.

According to Sujatha Jesudason of the Center for Genetics and Society, the groups that attended that retreat were enthusiastic about continuing the conversations within their own organizations and forming coalitions to address the issue. The pro-choice advocates in particular started a process of reflection on the tensions—between individual liberties and social justicer—that are especially prominent in their movement.

Creating a Coalition

In contemplating regulation, an example from the past might prove illuminating. In 1975, in New York, a multiracial coalition called the Advisory Committee on Sterilization helped implement guidelines for regulating sterilization, including a mandatory waiting period. The aim was to ensure informed consent, because so many poor minority women had been sterilized without it, in haste. Planned Parenthood and NARAL opposed the restrictions, arguing that they infringed on reproductive freedom. (White women, who frequently could not persuade doctors to sterilize them, did not want to make the process more cumbersome.) This conflict was perhaps the clearest manifestation of the discordant outlooks of different feminists.

The opposition of the mainstream groups was understandable, but it also reflected a degree of myopia. Likewise, Margaret Sanger was so single-minded in the promotion of her cause that she endorsed wrongheaded ideas that she believed would serve it. Now, we who support abortion rights may fear that regulating reproductive technologies could endanger our cause. There is no doubt that maintaining the legality of abortion—and fighting to reverse harmful restrictions of it—is paramount. But it is also important for us to sustain a larger moral vision. We have to find a way to advance that multifaceted program, including views on reproductive technologies, while protecting the right to abortion.

It appears inevitable that genetic technologies of all kinds will become one of the major issues of this century. It appears equally inevitable that the pro-choice movement will become entangled in the debate. In this new challenge, Margaret Sanger provides an instructive example—today's reproductive-rights advocates should emulate her passionate advocacy and avoid repeating her mistakes.

Organizations to Contact

The editors have compiled the following list of organizations concerned with the issues debated in this book. The descriptions are derived from materials provided by the organizations. All have publications or information available for interested readers. The list was compiled on the date of publication of the present volume; the information provided here may change. Be aware that many organizations take several weeks or longer to respond to inquiries, so allow as much time as possible.

Alan Guttmacher Institute

125 Maiden Ln., 7th floor, New York, NY   10038
(800) 355-0244 • fax: (212) 248-1951
e-mail (online form): www.guttmacher.org/about/info.php
Web site: www.guttmacher.org

The Alan Guttmacher Institute addresses sexual and reproductive health in the United States and worldwide through social science research, policy analysis, and public education. The institute produces a wide range of resources on topics pertaining to sexual and reproductive health, including *International Perspectives on Sexual and Reproductive Health*, formerly known as *International Family Planning Perspectives*; the *Guttmacher Policy Review*; and *Perspectives on Sexual and Reproductive Health*.

Americans United for Life (AUL)

310 S. Peoria St., Suite 500, Chicago, IL   60607
(312) 568-4700 • fax: (312) 568-4747
e-mail (online form): www.aul.org/Contact_AUL
Web site: www.aul.org

Americans United for Life (AUL) is a nonprofit, public-interest law and policy organization whose vision is a nation in which everyone is welcomed in life and protected in law. The first national pro-life organization in America, AUL has defended pro-life principles through judicial, legislative, and educational efforts since 1971. AUL publishes *Defending Life: Proven Strategies for a Pro-life America.*

Center for Reproductive Rights

120 Wall St., New York, NY   10005
(917) 637-3600 • fax: (917) 637-3666
e-mail: info@reprorights.org
Web site: http://reproductiverights.org

The Center for Reproductive Rights is a global legal advocacy organization dedicated to reproductive rights, with expertise in both U.S. constitutional and international human rights law. The center advances reproductive freedom as a fundamental human right, advocating a woman's freedom to decide whether and when to have children and seeking to protect her access to reproductive health care, including birth control, safe abortion, prenatal and obstetric care, and unbiased information. The center produces numerous books, reports, briefing papers, and fact sheets, including *Defending Human Rights* and *Bringing Rights to Bear: Abortion and Human Rights.*

Christian Defense Coalition

PO Box 77168, Washington, DC   20013
(202) 547-1735
e-mail: revmahoney@aol.com
Web site: www.christiandefensecoalition.com

The Christian Defense Coalition is a nationwide Christ-centered ministry committed to bringing governmental policies in line with biblical teachings, specifically in building a "culture of life" with a focus on abortion, human cloning, embryonic stem cell research and bioethics. The coalition also embraces social justice concerns such as poverty, racism, homelessness, human trafficking, prison reform, creation care (environmentalism), and other public policy issues. The coalition's Web site includes a blog, videos, and other information.

Focus on the Family
8605 Explorer Dr., Colorado Springs, CO   80920
(800) A-FAMILY (232-6459) • fax: (719) 531-3424
Web site: www.focusonthefamily.com

Focus on the Family is a nonprofit Christian evangelical organization founded in 1977 by family psychologist James Dobson to defend the institution of the family, promote biblical truths worldwide, and spread the Gospel of Jesus Christ. Focus on the Family partners with Christianbook.com to offer books, CD-ROMS, and DVDs on many topics, including abortion. The organization also publishes *Focus on the Family Citizen* magazine.

**NARAL Pro-Choice America and NARAL
Pro-Choice America Foundation**
1156 Fifteenth St. NW, Suite 700, Washington, DC   20005
(202) 973-3000 • fax: (202) 973-3096
e-mail (online form): www.prochoiceamerica.org/
feedback.html
Web site: www.prochoiceamerica.org/

Since 1969, NARAL Pro-Choice America has been a leading advocate for privacy and a woman's right to choose, working to develop and sustain a pro-choice political constituency in order to maintain the right of all women to legal abortion and access to reproductive health care. The nonprofit organization briefs members of Congress and testifies at hearings on abortion and related issues. NARAL publishes a monthly e-newsletter, *Choice and Change.*

National Abortion Federation (NAF)
1660 L St. NW, Suite 450, Washington, DC   20036
(202) 667-5881 • fax: (202) 667-5890
e-mail: naf@prochoice.org
Web site: http://prochoice.org

The National Abortion Federation (NAF) is the professional association of abortion providers in the United States and Canada. Its members believe that women should be trusted to make private medical decisions in consultation with their health-care provider. NAF offers training and services to abortion providers as well as unbiased, medically accurate information and referral services to women. NAF publishes numerous resources covering a wide range of subjects related to abortion for health-care providers, medical educators, patients, and the public, including the quarterly *Clinicians for Choice* e-newsletter and the publications *Having an Abortion? Your Guide to Good Care* and *Unsure About Your Pregnancy? A Guide to Making the Right Decision for You.*

National Organization for Women (NOW)
1100 H St. NW, 3rd floor, Washington, DC   20005
(202) 628-8669 • fax: (202) 785-8576
e-mail (online form): www.now.org/comments.html
Web site: www.now.org/issues/abortion

Founded in 1966, the National Organization for Women (NOW) is a large feminist advocacy group that seeks to bring about equality for all women. NOW's top six priority issues are advancing reproductive freedom, promoting diversity and ending racism, stopping violence against women, winning lesbian rights, achieving constitutional equality, and ensuring economic justice. NOW produces the national *NOW Times* newspaper and sponsors a national conference.

National Right to Life Committee (NRLC)
512 Tenth St. NW, Washington, DC   20004
(202) 626-8800
e-mail: nrlc@nrlc.org
Web site: www.nrlc.org

The National Right to Life Committee (NRLC) was founded in 1973 in response to the U.S. Supreme Court decision of *Roe v. Wade,* which legalized abortion in all fifty states. It is one of the largest organizations opposing abortion and has helped to achieve a number of legislative reforms at the national level. The group's ultimate goal is to provide legal protection to prenatal human life. NRLC publishes a monthly newspaper, the *National Right to Life News.*

Operation Rescue

PO Box 782888, Wichita, KS 67278-2888
(316) 683-6790 • fax: (916) 244-2636
e-mail: info@operationrescue.org
Web Site: www.operationrescue.org

Operation Rescue is an outspoken, antiabortion Christian activist organization that promotes direct action to restore legal personhood to the unborn and stop abortion in obedience to biblical mandates. Some of its tactics include blocking access to abortion clinics and showing graphic images of aborted fetuses on traveling "Truth Trucks." Publications include *Their Blood Cries Out* and *The Tiller Report.*

Planned Parenthood Federation of America (PPFA)

434 W. Thirty-third St., New York, NY 10001
(212) 541-7800 • fax: (212) 245-1845
e-mail (online form): www.plannedparenthood.org/about-us/contact-us.htm
Web site: www.plannedparenthood.org

Founded in 1916, Planned Parenthood Federation of America is a national organization that supports each individual's right to make informed, independent decisions about health, sex, and family planning. It provides contraception, abortion, reproductive health care, sex education, and information at health centers throughout the United States. Among its extensive publications are the pamphlets *The Facts of Life: A Guide for Teens and Their Families, Thinking About Abortion: Questions and Answers,* and *Your Contraceptive Choices.*

For Further Research

Books

Jacques Berlinerblau, *Thumpin' It: The Use and Abuse of the Bible in Today's Presidential Politics*. Louisville, KY: Westminster/ John Knox, 2008.

Joseph Bernardin, *The Seamless Garment: Writings on the Consistent Ethic of Life*. Maryknoll, NY: Orbis Books, 2008.

Simone M. Caron, *Who Chooses? American Reproductive History Since 1830*. Gainesville: University Press of Florida, 2008.

Robert F. Cochran Jr., ed., *Faith and Law: How Religious Traditions from Calvinism to Islam View American Law*. New York: New York University Press, 2008.

Alesha E. Doan, *Opposition and Intimidation: The Abortion Wars and Strategies of Political Harassment*. Ann Arbor: University of Michigan Press, 2007.

Nancy Ehrenreich, ed., *The Reproductive Rights Reader: Law, Medicine, and the Construction of Motherhood*. New York: New York University Press, 2008.

Krista Jacob, *Abortion Under Attack: Women on the Challenges Facing Choice*. Emeryville, CA: Seal Press, 2006.

Ellie Lee, *Abortion, Motherhood, and Mental Health: Medicalizing Reproduction in the United States and Great Britain*. New York: Aldine de Gruyter, 2003.

Carol Levine, *Taking Sides: Clashing Views on Bioethical Issues*. Guilford, CT: McGraw Hill, 2008.

Paul Benjamin Linton, *Abortion Under State Constitutions: A State-by-State Analysis*. Durham, NC: Carolina Academic Press, 2008.

Rachel M. MacNair and Stephen Zunes, eds., *Consistently Opposing Killing: From Abortion to Assisted Suicide, the Death Penalty, and War.* Westport, CT: Praeger, 2008.

Susan A. Martinelli-Fernandez, Lori Baker-Sperry, and Heather McIlvaine-Newsad, eds., *Interdisciplinary Views on Abortion: Essays from Philosophical, Sociological, Anthropological, Political, Health and Other Perspectives.* Jefferson, NC: McFarland, 2009.

J.K. Mason, *The Troubled Pregnancy: Legal Wrongs and Rights in Reproduction.* Cambridge: Cambridge University Press, 2007.

Eileen E. Morrison and John F. Monagle, *Health Care Ethics: Critical Issues for the 21st Century.* Sudbury, MA: Jones and Bartlett, 2009.

Ziad W. Munson, *The Making of Pro-life Activists: How Social Movement Mobilization Works.* Chicago: University of Chicago Press, 2008.

Laura Reichenbach and Mindy Jane Roseman, eds., *Reproductive Health and Human Rights: The Way Forward.* Philadelphia: University of Pennsylvania Press, 2009.

Jon A. Shields, *The Democratic Virtues of the Christian Right.* Princeton, NJ: Princeton University Press, 2009.

Helena Silverstein, *Girls on the Stand: How Courts Fail Pregnant Minors.* New York: New York University Press, 2007.

James D. Slack, *Abortion, Execution, and the Consequences of Taking Life.* New Brunswick, NJ: Transaction, 2009.

Agneta Sutton, *Christian Bioethics: A Guide for the Perplexed.* New York: T&T Clark, 2008.

Periodicals

David Barstow, "An Abortion Battle, Fought to the Death," *New York Times*, July 25, 2009.

Joseph Bottum, "And the War Came," *First Things*, June/July 2009.

Diana Buccafurni and Pepe Lee Chang, "Does Prenatal Diagnosis Morally Require Provision of Selective Abortion?" *American Journal of Bioethics*, August 2009.

A. Coghlan, "Pro-choice? Pro-life? No Choice," *New Scientist*, October 20, 2007.

Beth Dawes, "I Had an Abortion," *Teen Magazine*, February 1997.

Laia Font-Ribera, "Socioeconomic Inequalities in Unintended Pregnancy and Abortion Decision," *Journal of Urban Health*, January 2008.

Nancy Gibbs, "Tiller's Murder: The Logic of Extremism on Abortion," *Time*, June 2, 2009.

———, "Understanding America's Shift on Abortion," *Time*, May 19, 2009.

Joe Klein, "Hot Buttons," *Time*, June 15, 2009.

Sarah Kliff, "The Abortion Evangelist," *Newsweek*, August 31, 2009.

Anuradha Kumar, Leila Hessini, and Ellen M.H. Mitchell, "Conceptualising Abortion Stigma," *Culture, Health & Sexuality*, August 2009.

Jeannie Ludlow, "The Things We Cannot Say: Witnessing the Traumatization of Abortion in the United States," *Women's Studies Quarterly*, Spring/Summer 2008.

Marie Claire, "What Would You Do?" September 2009.

Sheelagh McGuinness, "Abortion: Prohibitions and Exceptions," *American Journal of Bioethics*, August 2009.

Steven C. Moore, "A Tragic Inheritance," *America*, February 16, 2009.

Gina Morgano, "A Baby or 'The Product of Your Conception'—One-Third of American Women Have an Abortion by Age 45," *Medill*, July 20, 2009.

Barack Obama, "Finding a Middle Ground: Remarks by the President in Commencement Address at the University of Notre Dame," *Vital Speeches of the Day*, July 2009.

Cynthia J. Patel, "Gender Role Attitudes and Attitudes to Abortion: Are There Gender Differences?" *Social Science Journal*, September 2009.

Katha Pollitt, "Dr. George Tiller, 1941–2009," *Nation*, June 29, 2009.

Nicolette Priaulx, "Rethinking Progenitive Conflict: Why Reproductive Autonomy Matters," *Medical Law Review*, Summer 2008.

John H. Richardson, "The Last Abortion Doctor," *Esquire*, August 5, 2009.

Gregg Sangillo, "Abortion's Shaky Middle Ground," *National Journal*, August 7, 2009.

Jon A. Shields, "What Abortionist Killers Believe," *Weekly Standard*, June 22, 2009.

Andrea Smith, "Beyond Pro-choice Versus Pro-life: Women of Color and Reproductive Justice," *NWSA Journal*, Spring 2005.

Sandra Steingraber, "The Story About the One," *Orion*, July/August 2009.

Ellen Wiebe, "Women's Perceptions About Seeing the Ultrasound Picture Before an Abortion," *European Journal of Contraception & Reproductive Health Care*, April 2009.

F.M. Wiecko, "Every Life Is Sacred . . . Kind Of: Uncovering the Sources of Seemingly Contradictory Public Attitudes Toward Abortion and the Death Penalty," *Social Science Journal*, December 2008.

Gail Williams, "Intimate Partner Violence, Pregnancy and the Decision for Abortion," *Issues in Mental Health Nursing*, April 2009.

Gabriel Winant, "O'Reilly's Campaign Against Murdered Doctor," *Salon*, May 31, 2009. www.salon.com.

Christina Zampas, "Abortion as a Human Right—International and Regional Standards," *Human Rights Law Review*, vol. 8, no. 2, 2008.

Index